ESSENTIAL

Essays by The Minimalists

JOSHUA FIELDS MILLBURN
& RYAN NICODEMUS

ASYM
METR
ICAL

Asymmetrical Press
Missoula, Montana

Published by Asymmetrical Press.

Let it go. It's just stuff.

Feel free to take pieces of this book and replicate them online or in print, but please link back to theminimalists.com. If you want to use more than a few paragraphs, that's great—please email themins@themins.com. If you illegally downloaded this book or stole a paperback version from the library or something, then shame on you! But please at least share your lifted copy with a friend or an enemy or anyone who might benefit from its words.

Library of Congress Cataloging-in-Publication Data
Essential: essays by the minimalists / Millburn, Nicodemus — 2nd ed.
Print ISBN: 978-1938793011
eISBN: 978-1936539451
WC: 67,761
1. Minimalism. 2. Happiness. 3. The Minimalists.
4. Simplicity. 5. Consumerism.

Photography by Joshua Weaver
Cover design by Dave LaTulippe, SPYR Media
Typeset in Avenir by Shawn Mihalik
Edited by Shawn Harding
Formatted in beautiful Montana
Printed in the U.S.A.

Author info:
Publisher: asymmetrical.co/jfm
Fiction: joshuafieldsmillburn.com
Essays: theminimalists.com
Email: themins@themins.com

ASYM METR ICAL

BOOKS BY THE MINIMALISTS

NONFICTION
Essential
Minimalism
Everything That Remains

FICTION
As a Decade Fades

For Stan & Kelly

Simplicity is the ultimate sophistication.

—Leonardo da Vinci

CONTENTS

CHAPTER ONE || MINIMALISM _____ 1

    Inside the Prison Walls of Consumerism _____ 3

    What Is Minimalism? _____ 4

    The Irony of Minimalism _____ 5

    Simple Isn't Radical _____ 6

    Is Minimalism Only for Single White Guys? ____ 7

    The Gospel of Less _____ 8

    About The Minimalists _____ 10

    About This Book _____ 12

    Constructing an Extraordinary Life _____ 13

    Whom This Book Is For _____ 14

    Not Utopia, but a Better World _____ 15

CHAPTER TWO || STUFF _____ 17

    Consumption Is Not the Problem _____ 19

    You Are What You Desire _____ 20

    The Rats in the Tunnel _____ 20

    Adequate _____ 22

    How We Woke Up _____ 23

    Haunted by Desire _____ 24

    In Too Deep _____ 25

    Minimalism Scares the Shit Out of Me _____ 26

    Decluttering Doesn't Work Like That _____ 27

    Organizing Is Well-Planned Hoarding _____ 29

    A Short Guide to Getting Rid of Your Crap ___ 30

    A Well-Edited Life _____ 33

    You Are Not Impressing Me _____ 34

    I Counted All My Stuff _____ 35

Start with the Easy Stuff _____ 37

Letting Go of Sentimental Items _____ 38

Packing Party: Unpack a Simpler Life _____ 41

Photo-Scanning Party _____ 47

Getting Rid of Just-In-Case Items _____ 48

90/90 Rule _____ 49

When Everything Is Your Favorite Thing _____ 50

Favorite Clothes of a Minimalist _____ 51

Spill Bleach on Your Wardrobe? _____ 52

Things We Walk Away From _____ 54

Home Is Where the Red Phone Is _____ 56

I Don't Love You Anymore _____ 58

A Rolex Won't Give You More Time _____ 59

I Got Rid of 2,000 Books _____ 61

Letting Go of Your DVD Collection _____ 63

More Is Less? _____ 65

CHAPTER THREE || TECHNOLOGY _____ 69

A Minimalist Approach to Technology _____ 71

Digital Clutter Is Different _____ 72

Shifting to a Culture of Access _____ 74

Don't Upgrade _____ 76

Reprogramming the Twitch _____ 77

Sleep, Sex, and Reruns _____ 80

Can I Get Him to Stop Watching TV? _____ 81

Check Email Like a Minimalist _____ 83

Deleting Music You No Longer Listen To ____ 85

Online Congruency _____ 87

CHAPTER FOUR || FINANCES _____ 89

A Minimalist's Thoughts on Money _____ 91

Money and Poverty Don't Buy Happiness ____ 94
Money Does Not Buy Better Habits _____ 95
Stimulate the Economy Like a Minimalist ____ 96
Fool Price _____ 98
Need, Want, Like _____ 99
Financial Freedom _____ 102
11 Signs You Might Be Broke _____ 109
Important Things We Put Off _____ 112
Can't Fix the Problem with the Problem ____ 114

CHAPTER FIVE || MINDFULNESS _____ 117
The Worst Thing That Could Happen _____ 119
Declutter Your Mental Clutter _____ 121
Fighting the Voice in Your Head _____ 124
How to Start Meditating _____ 129
Sam Harris Discusses Mindfulness _____ 130
5 Ways to Create Solitude _____ 137
A Quiet Place _____ 139
Alone Time _____ 141
Channel Surfing _____ 143
Forever Does Not Exist _____ 144
The Troubling Nature of Pop Culture _____ 145
Costs and Benefits of Awareness _____ 147
Offbeat _____ 148
Overcoming Self-Doubt _____ 150

CHAPTER SIX || GIFT-GIVING _____ 153
When to Give Gifts _____ 155
Gift Experiences, Not Stuff _____ 156
Letting Go of Physical Gifts _____ 157
The Commodification of Love _____ 158

An Irresponsible Christmas _ _ _ _ _ _ _ _ _ _ _ _ _ 160

Let's Talk About Black Friday _ _ _ _ _ _ _ _ _ _ _ 161

40 Reasons to Avoid Black Friday _ _ _ _ _ _ _ _ 162

Ask for Better Christmas Presents _ _ _ _ _ _ _ _ 164

The Worst Christmas Ever _ _ _ _ _ _ _ _ _ _ _ _ _ 165

CHAPTER SEVEN || PRIORITIES _ _ _ _ _ _ _ _ _ _ _ _ _ _ 167

Real Priorities _ 169

Not Busy, Focused _ _ _ _ _ _ _ _ _ _ _ _ _ _ _ _ _ 170

Killing Time _ 172

Your Own Advice Is the Hardest Pill _ _ _ _ _ _ 174

The Right Path, Left Path, and No Path _ _ _ _ _ 175

The End Is Right Past the Horizon _ _ _ _ _ _ _ _ 176

What Is My Outcome? _ _ _ _ _ _ _ _ _ _ _ _ _ _ _ 177

WWJD: What Would Joshua Do? _ _ _ _ _ _ _ _ _ 182

The Rules We Live By _ _ _ _ _ _ _ _ _ _ _ _ _ _ _ _ 183

Direction _ 184

Moving Beyond Goals _ _ _ _ _ _ _ _ _ _ _ _ _ _ _ 186

The Discomfort Zone _ _ _ _ _ _ _ _ _ _ _ _ _ _ _ _ 187

Killing the Internet at Home _ _ _ _ _ _ _ _ _ _ _ 188

Letting Go of Vacation Photos _ _ _ _ _ _ _ _ _ _ 192

Prime Optimist _ _ _ _ _ _ _ _ _ _ _ _ _ _ _ _ _ _ _ 194

CHAPTER EIGHT || HEALTH _ _ _ _ _ _ _ _ _ _ _ _ _ _ _ _ 197

Health Is a Vehicle, Not a Destination _ _ _ _ _ _ 199

A Minimalist's Thoughts on Diet _ _ _ _ _ _ _ _ _ 201

18-Minute Minimalist Exercises _ _ _ _ _ _ _ _ _ 205

Simple Triggers _ _ _ _ _ _ _ _ _ _ _ _ _ _ _ _ _ _ _ 208

The Taste of Health _ _ _ _ _ _ _ _ _ _ _ _ _ _ _ _ _ 209

CHAPTER NINE || RELATIONSHIPS _ _ _ _ _ _ _ _ _ _ _ 213

Walk a Mile in My Blisters _____215

Meaningful Relationships _____217

It's Complicated _____219

More Wins than Losses _____220

Building Your Trust Muscle _____221

Asking Others to Embrace Change _____222

Letting Go of Shitty Relationships _____226

Goodbye Fake Friends _____228

Know Thy Neighbor _____230

7 Ways to Meaningful Conversations _____232

You Don't Have to Explain Yourself _____234

Ending the Tyranny of Cool _____235

Hey, Look at Me! I'm Relevant, Dammit! ____237

Everyday Minimalists _____238

CHAPTER TEN || PASSION _____241

UnAmerican Dream _____243

Unteachers _____244

Life's Most Dangerous Question _____246

What Is Your Mission? _____249

"Follow Your Passion" Is Crappy Advice ____250

Too Much Branding These Days _____254

The Problem with Corporations _____256

Not Hereditary _____257

Create Your Masterpiece _____259

The Details _____263

Cola and Politics _____265

Course Correction _____266

CHAPTER ELEVEN || CONTRIBUTION _____269

Adding Value _____271

Ask Not What You Can Get _ _ _ _ _ _ _ _ _ _ _ _ _ 272

Here, Have an Organ _ _ _ _ _ _ _ _ _ _ _ _ _ _ _ _ 273

Repaying Intellectual Debt _ _ _ _ _ _ _ _ _ _ _ _ 275

CHAPTER TWELVE || SUCCESS _ _ _ _ _ _ _ _ _ _ _ _ 277

The Success Template _ _ _ _ _ _ _ _ _ _ _ _ _ _ _ 279

Life Is an Acquired Taste _ _ _ _ _ _ _ _ _ _ _ _ _ 281

The Right Kind of Fame _ _ _ _ _ _ _ _ _ _ _ _ _ _ 283

If, Then _ 287

Who to Emulate? _ _ _ _ _ _ _ _ _ _ _ _ _ _ _ _ _ _ 288

A Minimalist, a Cowboy, and an American _ _ 289

There Will Be Bruises _ _ _ _ _ _ _ _ _ _ _ _ _ _ _ 292

Worthy _ 293

Elementary School and Grad School _ _ _ _ _ _ 294

30 Life Lessons from 30 Years _ _ _ _ _ _ _ _ _ _ 296

I Will Always Be Okay _ _ _ _ _ _ _ _ _ _ _ _ _ _ _ 302

Fight Club's Tyler Durden Is a Minimalist _ _ _ 303

Jefferson's 10 Rules for a Good Life _ _ _ _ _ _ _ 306

Life After the Crash _ _ _ _ _ _ _ _ _ _ _ _ _ _ _ _ 308

Live Like Stan _ 309

ESSENTIAL

CHAPTER ONE || **Minimalism**

INSIDE THE PRISON WALLS OF CONSUMERISM

There's a shopping mall in San Diego that used to be a prison. Restored, repurposed, and redecorated, it's hard to imagine this place once imprisoned hundreds of inmates.

One might argue, however, it's a different kind of prison now: a voluntary incarceration, caged by the invisible walls of consumption.

This might sound hyperbolic, but it's an apt analogy.

Consumption isn't the problem: compulsory consumption is. We've trapped ourselves by thinking consumerism will make us happy—that buying crap we don't need will somehow make us whole.

We've gotten good at fooling ourselves, too. We've overdecorated the jailhouse walls—walls we've built around ourselves—and we've made our cells so comfortable we're terrified to leave: but a prison cell with a view is still a prison cell.

Perhaps there's a key to our escape.

WHAT IS MINIMALISM?

At first glance, people might think the point of minimalism is only to get rid of material possessions: Eliminating. Jettisoning. Extracting. Detaching. Decluttering. Paring down. Letting go.

That's a mistake, though.

Removing the excess is an important part of the recipe—but it's just one ingredient. If we're concerned solely with the stuff, then we're missing the larger point.

Minimalists don't focus on having less, less, less. Rather, we focus on making room for more, more, more: more time, more passion, more experiences, more growth, more contribution, more contentment—and more freedom. It just so happens that clearing the clutter from life's path helps us make that room.

Minimalism is the thing that gets us past the things so we can make room for life's important things—which actually aren't things at all.

There are many flavors of minimalism: A 20-year-old single guy's minimalist lifestyle looks different from a 45-year-old mother's minimalist life. Even though everyone embraces minimalism differently, each path leads to the same place: a life with more meaning.

THE IRONY OF MINIMALISM

A word of warning as you consider simplifying your life: If you call yourself a minimalist, or if you tell people you are interested in minimalism, then everything you do will instantly be steeped in irony.

Oh, you drive a car? That's not very minimalist of you! Wait, you have more than one pair of shoes? Hypocrite! You own a blowdryer? Phony!

What these people don't understand, however, is minimalism is not about deprivation: It's about finding more value in the stuff you own. Minimalists do this by removing the superfluous, keeping only the possessions that serve a purpose or bring joy. Everything else goes by the wayside.

There is no *Minimalist Rulebook*: We're all different. The things that add value to one person's life may not add value to yours. So hold on to that hair straightener, those colorful socks, that collection of angel statuettes—but only if they are appropriate for *your* life.

People will judge. Let them. Judgment is but a mirror reflecting the insecurities of the person who's doing the judging.

SIMPLE ISN'T RADICAL

Sometimes people avoid minimalism because the word itself sounds extreme, radical, subversive. Afraid of stepping outside cultural boundaries, these people avoid simplifying their lives because they don't want the label: *minimalist*.

If *minimalism* seems too austere, then perhaps you can re-label your flavor of simplification. May we suggest any of the following *-isms*:

Enoughism
Essentialism
Selectivism
Curationism
Naturalism
Stoicism
Epicureanism
Appropriatism
Simplism
Lessism
Practicalism
Livingwithinyourmeansism

Call it whatever you want: no matter which *-ism* you favor, the important part is it helps you live with intention.

IS MINIMALISM ONLY FOR SINGLE, RICH, WHITE GUYS?

Someone in Montreal asked us this question. Granted, she posited it more congenially than written above, but, restated this way, we get to the heart of the matter.

We won't bother detailing the many examples that immediately torpedo this assumption—our friend Leo Babauta and his six kids, Tammy Strobel and her tiny house, Patrick Rhone and his family, et al.—none of whom are single, nor rich, nor white guys, and yet they all embrace a minimalist lifestyle. (Note: You can read more about minimalist families, including additional books and resources, at *TheMinimalists.com/children*.)

Let's look at the question from a broader perspective:

The Bureau of Labor Statistics shows that in today's economy "it's entirely possible for poor people to have much of the same material comforts—cars, televisions, computers, smartphones—as more affluent people, yet be trapped in low-paying jobs with little prospect of improvement." In other words, rich people and poor people can both be oppressed by the possessions they desire. However, poor people are considerably more stifled because of their lesser "prospect of improvement."

Perhaps minimalism is the "prospect of improvement": Whenever desire is greater than one's ability to attain, discontentment sets in. By mitigating our impulse to compulsively consume, however, we take back control of our desires—as well as our pocketbooks. According to the

New York Times, there is evidence that "money relieves suffering in cases of true material need. But when money becomes an end in itself, it can bring misery, too." Once our basic human needs are met, money doesn't buy happiness—and neither does poverty.

People with fewer resources, especially those with less money, can benefit *most* from minimalism: a minimalist lifestyle helps people determine what truly adds value to their lives.

This is even more important when our resources are limited: If we have less money, then we must be more intentional with how we spend it.

Simplification begets intentionality. Rich or poor, married or single, black or white, simplifying one's life can only benefit one's circumstances. The Stoics understood this— as did Thoreau, Gandhi, Jesus, and the Buddha.

It sure would be nice if everyone else did, too.

THE GOSPEL OF LESS

No, minimalism is not a religion.

Religion is a complicated and sensitive subject for many. Even though we don't typically speak or write about religion, its presence seems to loom over each event we host. Curiosity is natural, so it's inevitable: People often approach us and say things like, "It's wonderful to see two guys spreading Jesus Christ's message." Which is usually followed by another person saying, "It's great to see a couple Buddhists sharing their story." Or, "Did you know Muhammad was the original minimalist?"

In a well-written, but unfortunately titled, newspaper article in Tennessee, we were recently said to be "spreading the gospel of less"—the connotation of which is a bit troubling. Even more troubling was a radio host's take in Oklahoma City when he referred to us as the "L. Ron Hubbard of minimalism." (Thankfully he was joking.)

Whatever your religious beliefs, we have no spiritual advice for you. The beautiful thing about minimalism, though, is it works whether you're religious or not. We personally know minimalists who are Christian pastors, minimalists who are practicing Buddhists, minimalists who are atheists. We even know a minimalist rabbi.

Because minimalism is a lifestyle that helps people question what things add value to their lives, it applies to any religion—or no religion at all. In fact, the two of us hold radically different religious beliefs.

Our journeys toward simplicity, however, had nothing to do with religion; instead, it was a reaction to the discontentment we experienced after being steeped in consumerism for three decades.

We live in a world in which many people have different beliefs, different faiths. But God or no God, we can all live more deliberately.

ABOUT THE MINIMALISTS

For us—Joshua & Ryan—it all started with a lingering discontent. A few years ago, while approaching age 30, we had achieved everything that was supposed to make us happy: great six-figure jobs, nice cars, big houses with more bedrooms than inhabitants, pointless masses of toys, scads of superfluous stuff.

And yet with all that stuff, we weren't satisfied with our lives. We weren't happy. There was a gaping void, and working 70–80 hours a week for a corporation and buying even more stuff didn't fill the void: It only brought more debt and stress and anxiety and fear and loneliness and guilt and overwhelm and depression.

We didn't control our time, and we didn't control our lives.

So in 2010, we took back control using the principles of minimalism to focus on what's important.

On December 14, 2010, we started *TheMinimalists.com* as a way to share our story.

In 2011, we left our corporate careers at age 30 to pursue something more meaningful. After publishing our first book, *Minimalism: Live a Meaningful Life*—a book about the five pillars of minimalism—we began contributing to people through writing classes and private mentoring sessions.

We have been fortunate to establish an online audience of millions of readers, and our story has been featured in the *New York Times, Wall Street Journal, Forbes, USA Today,*

National Post, *Time* magazine, *Today* show, and hundreds of other media outlets (the *Boston Globe* referred to our story as "Henry David Thoreau, but with Wi-Fi"). We have spoken at Harvard Business School, Apple, and several large conferences (SXSW, TEDx, WDS), as well as many smaller venues, including colleges, corporate groups, libraries, soup kitchens, and various non-profit organizations. (Note: You can watch our TEDx Talk at TheMinimalists.com/tedx.)

Toward the end of 2012, we moved from our hometown, Dayton, Ohio, to a cabin outside Philipsburg, Montana, as a four-month experiment.

We followed this with a move in 2013 to beautiful Missoula, Montana, where we cofounded Asymmetrical Press, a publishing house for the indie at heart.

In 2014, we published a bestselling memoir, *Everything That Remains*, and donated a year of our lives to a 100-city tour, traveling the globe to share our message at more than 100 free events in eight countries.

As of this writing, our newest project, *Minimalism: A Documentary About the Important Things*, a feature-length film directed by Matt D'Avella—in association with Catalyst, Asymmetrical, and SPYR Media—is in post-production and will be in theaters and online soon (more details at MinimalismFilm.com).

This is only the radically condensed version of our story— included here not to impress anyone, but rather to establish a context for this book. Should you want to, you can read the full version of our minimalist journeys in our aforementioned memoir, *Everything That Remains*. This book, however, is different.

ABOUT THIS BOOK

Since we started our website, we have written hundreds—if not thousands—of essays about a wide array of topics, ranging from simple living and cultivating passion, to writing, publishing, entrepreneurship, health, relationships, personal growth, and contribution.

In that time, many people asked us to collect our favorite essays from the blog and organize them in book form, which resulted in three short essay collections early on: *The Minimalists* (2011), *Simplicity* (2012), and *A Day in the Life of a Minimalist* (2013). However, in an effort to simplify our catalog, we decided we should combine all three books, trim the fat from those collections, and add some of our most important recent essays.

Effectively, this book is the "Best of The Minimalists"—but it's not a *book* book: It's more like a well-curated website made available in print and ebook formats.

Collected here are the most relevant essays—some short, some long—from our website. Most of these essays were written by us together; however, in the cases in which an essay was written solo, it is accompanied by a byline crediting either Joshua or Ryan for its authorship.

Parsed into twelve important themes, this collection has been edited and organized into an order that creates an experience appreciably different from reading blog posts online. By bringing our best work together into one tome, we removed any obvious redundancies, although we intentionally kept certain necessary repetitions to reinforce important points (e.g., phrases such as "add value," "contribute beyond yourself," and "meaningful life," appear with some frequency throughout these pages, each time to reiterate our core principles).

However, these are *individual* essays. While we organized this book in a deliberate manner, it is not meant to function as a linear narrative; rather, this book is meant to serve as a conversation in two ways: first, as a continuous conversation between the authors (Joshua & Ryan) and the reader, and second, as a conversation starter between the reader and the people in their life.

Every essay that follows is a single, standalone ingredient. Our intent is to provide all the ingredients you need to create your own recipe for an extraordinary life.

CONSTRUCTING AN EXTRAORDINARY LIFE

An extraordinary life doesn't just happen. It is constructed, crafted, curated.

We ought not simply "go with the flow," then. Going with the flow is nice and easy for a while, riding the current wherever it might take us—but eventually everyone ends up at the same place: the rapids. And then, unprepared, we're in for a world of hurt.

Your two authors both have extraordinary lives: We're not ashamed to admit this. It wasn't always this way, though.

For the longest time our lives were unremarkable at best, miserable at worst. Too long we went with the flow; as a result, we were fat, in debt, and unfulfilled by the lives we were leading—lives filled with every conceivable type of clutter: mental clutter, emotional clutter, physical clutter. We had reached the rapids and were quickly headed for the falls.

Then we decided to change.

An extraordinary life—a life to be proud of—is a decision. Not a single decision, but a myriad of little decisions each day. Daily decisions about money and health and passion and contribution. One day at a time. These decisions add up until one day you look over your shoulder and realize you've created an extraordinary life.

WHOM THIS BOOK IS FOR

Your two authors have learned more than we ever dreamed throughout our journey into minimalism—and we're still learning. The most important lesson we've learned, though, is minimalism appeals to only one group of people: people with an open mind.

During our coast-to-coast travels, we've experienced a diverse group of people. Thousands of people have attended our events, from factory workers to CEOs, from attorneys to stand-up comics, from eleven-year-old boys to

83-year-old great-grandmothers, from every ethnicity to every socioeconomic background, from high-school dropouts to college professors, from marathon runners to people struggling to lose weight, from single moms to parents bringing their teenagers to hear about a simpler life.

Minimalism is applicable to anyone—anyone with an open mind. We're all searching for meaningful lives: You are not alone.

NOT UTOPIA, BUT A BETTER WORLD

No, minimalism will *not* solve all your problems.

Unfortunately, people sometimes believe the goal of simple living is to own as few possessions as possible: to declutter our homes, to organize our lives, and to clear our minds. Once we do this, we'll each find our utopia and bask in the glory of our newfound happiness, right?

Not exactly. Real life doesn't work this way.

Minimalism is not the end game—it is not the result. Chucking your material possessions does not necessarily equal happiness. You could get rid of all your stuff and still be miserable.

Getting rid of the excess in your life will, however, help you discover what does make you happy. (Hint: it's not your possessions—most of your possessions are actually in the way of your happiness.) It's much easier to find the path toward happiness once you've cleared the debris.

Minimalism will never lead you to your utopia—life will always have its moments of tedium, drudgery, sadness, and pain—but minimalism can lead you to a better life, one that's more exciting, fulfilling, satisfying, and rewarding.

You can start small, but it's worth getting started today.

After you read this book—which is organized to be read in small chunks, one essay at a time—you can find additional free resources, games, photos, podcasts, and videos to help you plan your journey at *TheMinimalists.com*.

Let's begin, shall we?

CHAPTER TWO || Stuff

CONSUMPTION IS NOT THE PROBLEM

We all need some stuff. Many of us take it too far, though: the average American household contains more than 300,000 possessions.

We have accumulated more than we need in hopes it'll make us happy in some hypothetical future. But it won't— we know this. Needing more will always lead to a pall of desire until we feel trapped by consumption.

Purchasing more stuff to make us happy—following consumerism's broken template—is the real issue, not consumption.

The solution, then, is to consume deliberately—to ignore the bullshit advertisements and determine what we need based on our own lives, not what we've been told we need.

We're all different: what we need is different for each of us.

YOU ARE WHAT YOU DESIRE

Every whole person has wants, cravings, aspirations. We all desire something. We don't, however, all have the *same* desires.

Some of us long to create something purposeful, to make a difference in the world, to eschew the so-called American Dream in favor of something better, something more deliberate, an experience-driven life of intentionality instead of a life pushed toward the wrong side of the consumption continuum.

On the other hand, some of us watch the luminous box flickering in our living rooms and yearn for the material things in its advertisements—the things that bring us stress, discontent, and often keep us tied to a particular income, which keeps us tied to jobs we don't love (or worse, jobs we hate)—all so we can obtain the shiny objects projected on the glowing rectangle.

In truth, most of us desire both: We desire the experiences *and* the stuff. Usually the latter gets in the way of the former: Too often our material desires get in the way of a more meaningful life. We are what we desire.

THE RATS IN THE TUNNEL

There is a light at the end of the tunnel: we all know this. Even when it's hard to find, we know it's there, just beyond the bend.

Finding the light isn't the hardest part of life's journey: it's dealing with what's hiding in the tunnel. What lurks in the darkness keeps us from focusing on the light.

Anytime we visit New York City, we might see oversized rats scurrying down the blackened train tracks below the subway platform. If we jump down and walk those tracks, we will find the light at the end of the subway tunnel—eventually.

Finding the light isn't what worries us: what worries us are the rats in the tunnel. We must contend with whatever stalks the darkness, what waits to trip us up and keep us from the light.

The rats are no different from the plethora of obstacles getting in our way every day—the mundane tasks, the banal distractions, the vapid, harmful ways we pacify ourselves.

Minimalism allows us to remove those obstacles and focus on the light; it allows us to shoo the rats from the tunnel and find the light more quickly. Minimalism allows us to swiftly exit the tunnel and avoid the malevolent, filthy creatures lurking in the darkness.

And the light is so much brighter when you get out of the tunnel.

What are your rats? What keeps you in the tunnel, hidden from the light? Shopping? Television? Internet? Debt? Clothes? Gadgets and consumer electronics? Overeating? Something else?

What can you get rid of to focus on the light? What can you remove from your life to make it more meaningful?

ADEQUATE

You are inadequate. At least that's what advertisers would like you to believe.

You bear witness to proof of your inadequacy every day: You see it on your TV, hear it on your radio, stare back at it on your computer screen and on highway billboards. There are plenty of messages all around you to reinforce your utter inadequacy.

If you're a male, you're not a real man unless you drink this brand of beer and eat this particular cut of meat and drive this brand of sport utility vehicle.

And if you're a female, you're not a real woman unless you squeeze into this size dress and don this shiny piece of jewelry and tote this purse with all the ostentatious C's or LV's on its leather exterior.

Then, and only then, will you feel adequate—or so they'd have you believe.

But when you obtain these things, what happens? Do you feel long-term adequacy? No, of course not. Your thirst for over-indulgent consumption isn't quenched when you obtain more material possessions—it's just the opposite: Your desire to consume increases; you've set the bar higher, and thus the threshold for future satisfaction is higher. It's a vicious cycle.

Consumption is an unquenchable thirst. You create that thirst, you manufacture the desire to consume more. Advertisers play their role, they help activate the desire you create, but ultimately the desire is yours to control. Once you realize you have control, you can break the cycle—you can avoid the continuous downward spiral.

There is one way out of consumption's spiral: We must realize the things we purchase do not define who we are—unless we allow them to.

If we are defined by our things, we will never be happy—but if we are defined by our actions, then we'll have the opportunity to feel fulfilled by our everyday growth, we'll have the opportunity to feel satisfied with our everyday contribution to others, and we'll have the opportunity to be content every day of our lives.

The stuff doesn't make you happy—*you* make you happy.

HOW WE WOKE UP

Every moth is drawn to light, even when that light is a flame—hot, burning, flickering—the fire tantalizing the drab creature with its bluish-white illumination. But when the moth flies too close to the flame, we all know what happens: It gets burned, incinerated by the very thing that drew it near.

For decades now, we consumers have been moths, lured by the blue flame of consumerism, pop culture's beautiful conflagration, a firestorm of lust and greed and wanting, a solipsistic desire to consume that which cannot be consumed, to be fulfilled by that which can never be fulfilling, a vacant proposition, leaving us empty inside, further fueling the blaze of lust and greed and wanting.

From our intimate vantage points, within reach of the flame's scorching edges, the fire seems impossible to extinguish. Unlike the moth, though, we have a choice. It is not an easy choice: The flame is ever more intriguing. Advertisers make sure of this: It is their job to find new ways to make the blaze eternally more appealing.

Some of us recognize a need for change. Others know change is necessary, but refuse to stop circling the mesmerizing flame—they can't remove their eyes from the spill of electric light illuminating their homes. Still others don't realize it's a flame at all—how could something so beautiful be so dangerous? So they circle the inferno, unconscious of its dangers.

We must, however, accept the flame for what it is: necessary, beautiful, and—most of all—dangerous. When we do this—when we step back to understand the nature of the fire—we have a chance to survive. This takes deliberate thought, repeated questioning of the way we live, a thorough understanding of why we feel comforted by the flame. It is difficult to do, but this is how we wake up.

HAUNTED BY DESIRE

The ghosts of desperation, lust, and envy hide in the shadow of our yearning: Be it money, material possessions, or accolades, we are haunted by our aspirations.

Covet that shiny new truck, that next big promotion, that beautiful man or woman, and you will feel unspeakable pain until it, he, or she is yours. When your desire is met, however, your flame is not extinguished—you're filled with new desires. It's a never-ending cycle.

The key, then, is to aspire toward something worthwhile. Instead of jonesing for things, we must pursue those which are without definitive milestones: growth, contribution, love.

These qualities are self-fulfilling: Seek growth and you will grow, endeavor to give to others and you will contribute, love others and your cup will overflow.

It is not wrong to have aspirations, desires, goals—but it is wrong for us to imagine we can ever satiate our ever-growing need for more.

IN TOO DEEP

It's easy to believe Earth turns slowly on its axis: It's always there; we're a part of it, deep in the middle of its rotation.

In many ways, consumerism is the same way: It's all around us, everywhere we turn, seemingly unstoppable—Hell's self-consuming heart.

But Earth doesn't turn slowly: It's spinning at over a thousand miles an hour. This became easy for us to understand once we stepped back and paid attention, once we became aware of our surroundings.

Similarly, we needn't look around at all this mass-consumption and over-indulgence and believe it's normal —it's not.

Things haven't always been this way—this chaotic, this meaningless—and the future needn't be, either. A sunrise is on the horizon, and we can see it once we open our eyes, become more aware of what's important, and realize we're in too deep.

MINIMALISM SCARES THE SHIT OUT OF ME
by Ryan Nicodemus

Minimalism scares the shit out of you. You're worried you'll get rid of stuff you'll need later. You're worried what your friends, your family, your co-workers, and your neighbors will think of you. You're worried you'll lose your identity, your status, and everything you've given meaning to in your life.

Me, too. Minimalism *still* scares the shit out of me.

I know there are many people who are as scared as me, and I'm here to tell you that's OK.

I have always been the type of person who puts his whole heart into his beliefs. When I take on a particular ideal or way of life, I make the most of it. I do this to a fault. I have such high expectations of myself that I often expect perfection, which is probably why I stress out easier than most, why I have more anxiety than most.

On top of the expectations, a lot of people around me love to point out every "non-minimal" thing I have in my life. They love to talk about how I own a condo, wear nice shoes, and have a nice haircut (yes, someone actually brought up my haircut), and the list goes on and on. But these people are only projecting. They feel as though I'm judging them because I don't live the way they do anymore.

You might be thinking, *Ryan, why do you care what people think?* It's not about my caring as much as these people reaffirming negative things I already think about myself (with the exception of my haircut, which I'm quite fond of, thank you very much). I'm aware there are many things in my life I still need to minimize. The simplifying process, like life, is ever-changing. Minimalism is fluid. As our circumstances change, our versions of the simple life must change, too.

The beautiful thing about minimalism is there is no right or wrong, there is no pace at which you must live your life, and there is nothing that says "this is how you have to live." Minimalism is a journey, and it is scary for everyone.

DECLUTTERING DOESN'T WORK LIKE THAT

Decluttering is, by and large, a farce. If you picked up this book to figure out how to declutter your closet, you're in the wrong place. You'll be hard-pressed to find anything here even vaguely resembling something as trite as "67 Ways to Declutter a Messy Home." That's because decluttering alone doesn't solve the problem: Discussing how to get rid of your stuff answers only the *what*, but not the *why*.

The *what*—i.e., the *how to*—is easy. We all know, instinctually, *how to* declutter. You can start small: Focus on one room at a time, making progress each day as you work toward a simplified life. You can go big: Rent a dumpster and throw out everything, moving on to a more fulfilling life. Or you can take the moderate approach: Plunge into a Packing Party and embrace the fun side of decluttering, enjoying the entire simplification process.

People should, however, be much more concerned with the *why*—the *purpose* behind decluttering—than the *what*. While the *what* is easy, the *why* is far more obscure because the nature of the *why* is highly individual. Ultimately, it has to do with the benefits *you'll* experience once you're on the other side of decluttering.

Decluttering is not the end result—it is merely the first step. You don't become instantly happy and content by just getting rid of your stuff—at least not in the long run. Decluttering doesn't work like that. If you simply embrace the *what* without the *why*, then you'll get nowhere (slowly and painfully, by the way, repeatedly making the same mistakes). It is possible to get rid of everything you own and still be utterly miserable, to come home to your empty house and sulk after removing all your pacifiers.

When you get rid of the vast majority of your possessions, you're forced to confront your darker side: *When did I give so much meaning to material possessions? What is truly important in life? Why am I discontent? Who is the person I want to become? How will I define my own success?*

These are difficult questions with no easy answers, but these questions are far more important than just ditching your material possessions: If you don't answer them carefully, rigorously, then the closet you just decluttered will be brimming with new purchases not long from now.

ORGANIZING IS WELL-PLANNED HOARDING

We need to start thinking of *organizing* as a dirty word. It is a sneaky little profanity that keeps us from simplifying our lives.

Our televisions would have us believe there's a battle being fought on the consumption continuum, a battle between the organizers and the hoarders—and from our couches it's hard to see who's winning.

We posit to you these two sides are working together, colluding to achieve the same thing: the accumulation of more stuff. One side—the hoarders—does so overtly, leaving everything out in the open, making them easy targets to sneer at. But the other side—the sneaky organizers—are more covert, more systematic, more devious when it comes to the accumulation of stuff. Ultimately, though, organizing is nothing more than well-planned hoarding.

Sure, both sides go about their hoarding differently, but the end result is not appreciably different. Whether our homes are strewn with wall-to-wall material possessions or we have a complex ordinal item-dispersal system, color-coded and alphabetized, we're still not dealing with the real problem.

No matter how organized we are, we must continue to care for the stuff we organize, cleaning and sorting our methodically structured belongings. When we get rid of the superfluous stuff, we can focus on life's more important aspects: we can spend the day focusing on our health, on our relationships, on pursuing our passions—or we can reorganize the basement again.

Once the excess stuff is out of the way, staying organized is much easier.

A SHORT GUIDE TO GETTING RID OF YOUR CRAP
by Joshua Fields Millburn & Julien Smith

Yay, it's Friday! Time to head home and relax after a week of hard work.

Step 1. Enter the front door of your home. Toss off your shoes. Notice, sitting behind the door, a pair of boots you have worn only once. Shrug.

Step 2. Turn on the television and sit on your IKEA couch. Attempt to relax. Awaken 20 minutes later, realizing you've been passively flipping through channels. Turn off the TV, remove the batteries from your remote. Toss them in your Blendtec blender. Stop yourself moments away from doing something drastic.

Step 3. Briefly fondle the iPhone in your pocket. Stop yourself, realizing you were about to do the exact same thing with YouTube as you just did with TV. Delete every unnecessary app from your phone.

Step 4. Wonder what people did before television and Internet access. Observe the room around you, looking over the unread books and unwatched DVDs lining your dusty shelves. Consider shopping, then picture the unworn clothes occupying your cavernous walk-in closet.

Step 5. Realize your imagination has turned all black and grey, the creativity drained from your life.

Step 6. Suddenly recognize you haven't used your "spare" room ... ever. Shit! Do the math and realize said room is costing you five or six hours of work per month. Take out a piece of paper and compare it to that trip to Europe you've been meaning to take. Stare at the math in disbelief. Stuff the paper in your mouth and begin to chew.

Step 7. Realize the brief emotional rush that accompanied the purchase of each item in your home is now gone, leaving only the object itself in its most basic, uninteresting form. The gorgeous, pastel designer couch has become simply a chair. A beautiful glass buffet is transformed into a mere table. A set of immaculate handmade dishes has aged into nothing but a bunch of plates. Your goose-down duvet is actually just a blanket. Wince.

Step 8. Glance down at your groceries and realize the Doritos, Lay's, and Ruffles you purchased are nothing but colored corn and potatoes.

Step 9. Open your credit-card bill. Wide-eyed, discover

how often you've confused shopping with actual extracurricular activities. Consider joining a monastery.

Step 10. Remember that time you went over to a party in a friend's loft. Recall the roommates, the self-made art and photos on the walls, the obscenely cheap rent, the happiness and simplicity of it all.

Step 11. Quickly create a list of the top ten things you own in terms of how much they cost. With horror, make a second list of the top ten things that make you happy. Sense the creeping dread as you realize there is no overlap between the two. Shudder.

Step 12. Decide to have a Packing Party like your friend suggested one time. Take the old sheets you never used from Crate & Barrel. Cover all your stuff with them. Endeavor not to uncover it unless you decide you need to use it. Suddenly realize you will never use anything because you are never home.

Step 13. Remember a time in childhood when you were more excited by ideas, love, travel, and people than by anything else. Realize you have, somehow, bought into a new religion, and that malls, from the inside, look exactly like cathedrals.

Step 14. Consider starting a fire.

Step 15. Consider that, perhaps, you are more than just your stuff. Begin to take a long walk. Breathe.

Step 16. Begin to relax. Give yourself the freedom to begin to dream again.

A WELL-EDITED LIFE
by Joshua Fields Millburn

Everyone develops their own creative process over time.

Some sculptors, Bernini for instance, build sculptures with clay. Others, like Michelangelo, carve from marble. Though I'm no Michelangelo, my creative process tends to mimic the latter, building way too much and then removing massive amounts of excess until I uncover the beauty beneath the banality.

I call this process Subtractive Creation. Unlike most carving sculptors, though, I also have to quarry the marble from which I pitch, chisel, and polish.

The essays on our website are published with around 400 words, even though they often start with 2,000 or more. My novel was 950 pages before it entered the world with only 252. The book you're reading now was 700 pages at its bloated apex; now it's fewer than half.

When I edit this way, the final result is far more meaningful to me, and to the reader. The care and handcraftedness shows in the final work. I teach my writing students how to edit this way, too; that is, how to spend one-third of their time writing effectively and two-thirds of their time editing, shaping their work into something more concise, more powerful, more beautiful.

Subtractive Creation seems to be an appropriate metaphor for the rest of life as well. There will always be life's excess, always more, always too many inputs bombarding us from every direction. But instead of abhorrent multitasking, instead of trying to get things done, we can make life more beautiful via subtraction.

We can filter out the noise. We can remove unnecessary material possessions. We can let go of sentimental items. We can get rid of negative relationships. We can avoid the American Dream. And when everyone is looking for more, we can focus on less.

Sure, there's an infinite amount of materials with which to build our lives—but sometimes the best way to build is to subtract. The best lives are often well-edited, carefully curated lives.

(P.S. Yes, I know Bernini also sculpted with marble.)

YOU ARE NOT IMPRESSING ME

Our Please-Like-Me culture has transformed into something hideous. We've been enveloped by an epidemic of pointless, attention-grabbing solipsism. Look around—the world is attempting to impress you.

We needn't impress anyone, and yet we all try. Relentlessly we try, doing the strangest things to get the attention and, ultimately, the approval of others.

Oh, you purchased a brand new Lexus? You're a published author? Your job title is X and you earn six-figures?

So what!

Take it from two guys who had it all: we had to get everything we ever wanted to realize that everything we ever wanted wasn't what we wanted at all. It was empty, meaningless, depressing.

Your material possessions, your social status, and even your so-called accomplishments don't impress anyone. They certainly don't impress us. *You* impress us—not the things around you. We are impressed by your commitment to change, by your ability to grow, by your desire to contribute beyond yourself. Everything else is just a social construct, devoid of meaning.

There's nothing inherently wrong with owning possessions, accomplishing goals, or earning money—just don't think those things impress anyone. They don't. At least not in a meaningful way.

I COUNTED ALL MY STUFF

The most unfortunate misconception we encounter about minimalism has to do with the act of counting your possessions.

"I could never be a minimalist, because I don't want to live with less than 100 things." We hear that a lot. Even well-regarded Internet stars inadvertently promulgate this misconception, saying odd things like, "I'm not a minimalist —I have no desire to move to a 300-square-foot apartment and religiously track the number of socks I own."

Yeah, neither do we.

Seeing people propagate such misconceptions is unfortunate because it gives an important movement a black eye and scares people away from something greater. Often the people promoting such ideas do so without malice, but they do so because they are afraid of labels—but some labels are helpful.

Minimalism has helped thousands of people discover meaning in their lives. It has never been about counting stuff. Even our friend Dave Bruno, the author of the *100 Thing Challenge*, would be the first person to attest to this. Dave lived for a long time with only 100 things (as a personal challenge), but the reason he did so was to prove our constant consumption is void of meaning, but the number of possessions is arbitrary.

As a parodic take on why counting isn't necessary, Joshua counted his stuff last year. That essay, "Everything I Own: My 288 Things" (TheMinimalists.com/288), is, ironically, one of the most popular essays on our site. The ostensible subject (counting your possessions) was not the true subject—it was not the point; the point was that taking a physical inventory of your life is eye-opening, and it helps you get rid of unnecessary items so you can appreciate what you have.

You don't have to count your stuff, although you can if you want. Either way, minimalism can help you live more and need less irrespective of how many pairs of socks you own.

START WITH THE EASY STUFF

Baffled by life's excess, we often look around at our piles of miscellanea and throw our hands in the air. There's so much emotion—so many memories—wrapped up in our possessions.

Although, of course, the memories aren't in the possessions—they're inside us—and that's where they'll always be.

But, still, letting go is difficult. Difficult, but not impossible.

Want to start simplifying? First, avoid sentimental items and difficult-to-part-with objects: You'll never get started if you're faced with all that heavy lifting. And stay away from the most onerous rooms: Basements, garages, and attics—they will only overwhelm you.

Instead, start with the easy things: The superfluous clothes jammed in the closet, the junk drawers teeming with junk, the unused kitchenware taking up space just in case.

If you begin with the things that are painless, then, as inertia takes over, simplifying gets easier by the day.

Moreover, the journey toward a simpler life is more enjoyable with an accountability partner. A new month is always peeking its head around the corner, which means it's the perfect time to play the 30-Day Minimalism Game (TheMinimalists.com/game). So grab a friend, clear the clutter, and have some fun together.

LETTING GO OF SENTIMENTAL ITEMS
by *Joshua Fields Millburn*

My mother died in 2009. She lived a thousand miles away, and it was my responsibility to vacate her apartment in Florida. It was a small, one-bedroom place, but it was packed wall-to-wall with her belongings. Mom had great taste—she could have been an interior designer—and none of her stuff was junk. Nevertheless, there was a lot of stuff in her home.

Mom was constantly shopping, always accumulating more stuff. She had antique furniture throughout her apartment, a stunning oak canopy bed that consumed almost her entire bedroom, two closets jam-packed with clothes, picture frames standing on every flat surface, original artwork adorning the walls, and tasteful decorations in every nook, cranny, and crevasse. There was 64 years of accumulation in that apartment.

So I did what any son would do: I rented a large truck from U-Haul. Then I called a storage place back in Ohio to make sure they had a big enough storage unit. The truck was $1600, the storage facility was $120—financially I could afford it, but I quickly found out the emotional cost was much higher.

At first I didn't want to let go of anything. If you've ever lost a parent, a loved one, or been through a similarly emotional time, then you understand exactly how hard it was for me to let go of any of those possessions. So instead of letting go, I wanted to cram every trinket, figurine, and piece of oversized furniture into that storage locker in Ohio. Floor to ceiling. That way I *knew* that Mom's stuff was there if I ever wanted it, if I ever needed access to it for some incomprehensible reason. I even planned to put a few pieces of Mom's furniture in my home as subtle reminders of her.

I started boxing up her belongings: every picture frame, every porcelain doll, and every white doily on every shelf. I packed every bit of her that remained.

Or so I thought.

I looked under her bed. Among the organized chaos that comprised the crawlspace beneath her bed, there were four boxes, each labeled with a number. Each numbered box was sealed with packing tape. I cut through the tape and found old papers from my elementary school days from nearly a quarter-century ago: spelling tests, cursive writing lessons, artwork—it was all there, every shred of paper from my first four years of school. It was evident she hadn't accessed the sealed boxes in years, yet Mom had held on to these things because she was trying to hold on to pieces of me, pieces of the past—much like I was attempting to hold on to pieces of *her* and *her* past.

I realized my retention efforts were futile. I could hold on to her memories without her stuff, just as she had always remembered me, my childhood, and all our memories without ever accessing those sealed boxes under her bed. She didn't need papers from 25 years ago to remember me, just as I didn't need a storage locker filled with her stuff to remember her.

I called U-Haul and canceled the truck. And then, over the next twelve days, I donated her stuff to places and people who could use it.

Of course it was difficult to let go, but I realized many things about our relationship between memories and possessions during the entire experience:

I am not my stuff; we are more than our possessions.
Our memories are within us, not within our things.
Holding on to stuff imprisons us; letting go is freeing.
You can take pictures of items you want to remember.
Old photographs can be scanned.
An item that is *sentimental* for us can be *useful* for someone else.

I don't think sentimental items are bad, or evil, or that holding on to them is wrong—I don't. I think the danger of sentimental items—and sentimentality in general—is far more subtle. If you want to get rid of an item but the only reason you are holding on to it is for sentimental reasons—if it is weighing on you—then perhaps it's time to get rid of it, perhaps it's time to free yourself of the weight. That doesn't mean you need to get rid of everything, though.

When I returned to Ohio, I had four boxes of Mom's photographs in my trunk, which I would later scan and back up online. I found a scanner that made scanning the photos easy (TheMinimalists.com/scanning). Those photos are digital now and they can be used in digital picture frames instead of collecting dust in a basement. I no longer have the clutter of their boxes lying around and weighing me down, and they can never be destroyed in a fire.

I donated everything else strewn throughout her home: her furniture, her clothes, and her decorative items. It was a giant leap for me, but I felt it must be done to remove the weight—the emotional *gravitas*—of the situation from my shoulders. I don't need Mom's stuff to remind me of her—there are traces of her everywhere: in the way I act, in the way I treat others, even in the way I smile. She's still there, and she was never part of her stuff.

Whenever I give advice on paring down, I tend to give two options:

The first option is usually the *giant leap* option, the dive-in-head-first option (e.g., get rid of everything, smash your TV, throw out all your stuff, quickly rip off the band-aid, etc.). This option isn't for everyone—and it's often not for me—but in this case, that's what I did. I donated everything.

The second option is to take *baby steps*—it works because it helps you build momentum by taking action. What sentimental item can you get rid of today that you've wanted to get rid of for a while? Start there. Then pick one or two things per week and gradually increase your efforts as you feel more comfortable.

Whichever option you choose, take action—never leave the scene of a good idea without taking action.

PACKING PARTY: UNPACK A SIMPLER LIFE
by Ryan Nicodemus

What makes a rich person rich? When I was a teenager, I thought it was $50,000 a year. When I started climbing the corporate ladder in my early twenties, I soon earned 50 grand. Something was wrong, though—I didn't feel rich.

So I went back to the drawing board and discovered my error: I forgot to adjust for inflation. Maybe $75,000 a year was rich. Maybe $90,000. Maybe six figures. Or maybe owning a bunch of stuff—maybe that was rich.

Whatever rich was, I knew that once I got there, I'd finally be happy. So as I made more money, I spent more money—all in the pursuit of the American Dream. All in the pursuit of happiness. But the closer I got, the further away happiness was.

Five years ago, my life was different from what it is today. Radically different. I had everything I ever wanted, everything I was "supposed" to have: I had an impressive job title at a respectable corporation—a successful career managing dozens of employees. I earned a six-figure income. I bought a shiny new car every few years. I owned a huge, three-bedroom, two-bathroom, two-thousand-square-foot condo. It even had two living rooms. (Other than maintaining several play rooms for my cat, I have no idea why a single guy needs two living rooms.)

My cat and I were living the American Dream. Everyone around me said I was successful—but I was only ostensibly successful. You see, I also had a bunch of things that were hard to see from the outside.

Even though I earned a lot of money, I had heaps of debt. Chasing the American Dream cost me a lot more than money: my life was filled with stress, anxiety, and discontent. I was miserable. I may have looked successful, but I certainly didn't feel successful. It got to a point where I didn't know what was important anymore. But one thing was clear: there was a gaping void in my life.

So I tried to fill that void the same way many people do: with stuff. Lots of stuff. I attempted to fill the void with consumer purchases. I bought new cars, new electronics, and new expensive clothes. I bought expensive furniture, home decorations, and all the latest gadgets. When I didn't have enough cash in the bank, I paid for expensive meals, rounds of drinks, and frivolous vacations with credit cards. I spent money faster than I earned it in an attempt to buy my way to happiness.

And I thought I'd get there one day. Happiness had to be just around the corner.

But the stuff didn't fill the void—it widened it. And because I didn't know what was important, I continued to fill the void with stuff, going further into debt, working hard to buy things that weren't making me happy. This went on for years—a demoralizing cycle.

By my late twenties, my life on the outside looked great—but inside, I was a mess. I was several-years divorced. I was unhealthy. I felt stuck. I drank—a lot. I did drugs—a lot. I used as many pacifiers as I could. And I continued to work 60, 70, sometimes 80 hours a week, forsaking the most important aspects of my life. I barely ever thought about my health, my relationships, my passions. Worst of all, I felt stagnant: I wasn't growing, and I certainly wasn't contributing to others.

My life lacked meaning—purpose—passion. If you would have asked me what I was passionate about, I would have looked at you like a deer in headlights. What am I passionate about? I had no idea.

I was living paycheck to paycheck. Living for a paycheck. Living for stuff. Living for a career I didn't love. I wasn't really *living* at all, though. I was depressed.

Then, as I was approaching age 30, I noticed something different about my best friend of 20 years: Josh seemed happy for the first time in a long time. Like, truly happy—ecstatic.

But why? We had worked side by side at the same corporation throughout our twenties, both climbing the ranks, and he had been just as miserable as me. Something significant had changed. To boot, he had just gone through two of the most difficult events of his life: his mother had just passed away, and his marriage had ended. Both in the same month. He wasn't supposed to be happy—and he definitely wasn't supposed to be happier than me.

So I did what any good friend would do: I bought him lunch at a fine-dining establishment (we went to Subway). While we were eating our sandwiches, I asked Josh: "Why the hell are you so happy?"

Josh spent the next 20 minutes telling me about something called minimalism. He talked about how he'd spent the last few months simplifying his life, getting the clutter out of the way to make room for what was truly important. And then he showed me an entire community of people who had done the same thing.

He introduced me to a guy named Colin Wright, a 24-year-old entrepreneur who travels to a new country every four months carrying with him everything he owns. Then there was Joshua Becker, a 36-year-old husband and father of two, with a full-time job and a car and a house in suburban Vermont. Next he showed me Courtney Carver, a 40-year-old wife and mother to a teenage daughter in Salt Lake City. And there was Leo Babauta, a 38-year-old husband and father of six in San Francisco.

Although all these people led considerably different lives, they all shared at least two things in common:

First, they were living deliberate, meaningful lives; they were passionate and purpose-driven; and they seemed much *richer* than any of the so-called rich guys I worked with in the corporate world.

Second, they all attributed their improved lives to this thing called minimalism.

So, being the problem solver I am, I decided to become a minimalist right there on the spot. I looked up at Josh and excitedly announced, "Alright, I'm in. I am a minimalist! Um…now what?"

You see, I didn't want to spend months slowly paring down my possessions like Josh had. That was fine for him, but I needed faster results. So we came up with a crazy idea: let's throw a Packing Party. (Everything is more fun when you put "party" at the end.) We decided to pack all my belongings as if I were moving, and then I would unpack only the items I needed over the next three weeks.

Josh came over and helped me box up everything: my clothes, my kitchenware, my towels, my electronics, my TVs, my framed photographs and paintings, my toiletries, even my furniture. Everything. We literally pretended I was moving.

After nine hours and a few pizza deliveries, everything was packed. There we were, sitting in my *second* living room, feeling exhausted, staring at boxes stacked halfway to my twelve-foot ceiling. My condo was empty and everything smelled like cardboard. Everything I owned—every single thing I had worked for over the past decade—was there in that room. Boxes stacked on top of boxes stacked on top of boxes.

Each box was labeled so I'd know where to go when I needed a particular item. Labels like, "living room," "junk drawer #1," "kitchen utensils," "bedroom closet," "junk drawer #7." And so on.

I spent the next 21 days unpacking only the items I needed. My toothbrush. My bed and bedsheets. Clothes for work. The furniture I actually used. Kitchenware. A tool set. Just the things that added value to my life.

After three weeks, 80% of my stuff was still in those boxes. Just sitting there. Unaccessed. I looked at those boxes and I couldn't remember what was in most of them. All those things that were supposed to make me happy weren't doing their job.

So I sold some of it, and then donated the rest.

And you know what? I started to feel rich for the first time in my life. I felt rich once I got everything out of the way, so I could make room for everything that remains.

PHOTO-SCANNING PARTY
by Joshua Fields Millburn

If you're going to ask for one physical gift this year for the holidays, consider a good photo scanner.

If you're like me, then you've probably let the overstuffed boxes and photo albums go unchecked over the years, and now they're collecting dust in your basement or closet, unused, just sitting there, waiting for "one day" to come.

One day: two of the most dangerous words in the English language.

I, too, held on to heaps of meaningful photos that added no value to my life because they were hidden away, and the prospect of dealing with them seemed daunting, overwhelming, not worth the hassle. So I let them sit in the attic, the cupboard, the garage.

Then, inspired by Ryan's Packing Party, I decided to throw a Photo-Scanning Party. (It turns out that if you put "party" at the end of anything, Ryan will show up.)

First, I found a high-quality scanner (TheMinimalists.com/scanning) that allows me to rapidly feed photos and immediately save them to a memory card, which I could then use in a couple high-res digital picture frames. What a novel idea: actually display my treasured photos. Plus, if anything were to happen to my home—flood, fire, robbery —all my photos are backed up online; thus, I'll never worry about losing those memories. Of course, the memories aren't in our material possessions, but I've found that a well-curated photo collection can help trigger all the wonderful memories of yesteryear—without all the physical baggage.

Next, to make my "party" a little more fun—and less lonely —I invited a few friends over, ordered food and drinks, and together we thumbed through the photographs of my childhood and all of its double-chinned grandeur, scanning my favorites to display.

I have one remaining box of photos I'm going to scan this month. I think another Scanning Party is in order. Feel free to join me: Scan your own photos and share some of your favorites on Twitter or Instagram using our #ScanningParty hashtag.

GETTING RID OF JUST-IN-CASE ITEMS

We often hold on to things *just in case* we need them. We don't let go because we *might* need something in some far-off, nonexistent, hypothetical future. And we pack too much stuff for trips and vacations *just in case*.

We needn't hold on to these things just in case. The truth is, we rarely use our just-in-case items, and so they sit there, take up space, get in the way, weigh us down. Most of the time they aren't items we need at all.

Instead—if we remove the just-in-case items from our lives —we can get them out of the way, we can free up the space they consume.

Over the last few years, the two of us let go of the vast

majority of our just-in-case possessions. And during our last tour, we made sure we didn't pack anything *just in case*.

And then we tested our theory: the 20/20 Rule.

Anything we get rid of that we truly need, we can replace for less than $20 in less than 20 minutes from our current location. Thus far, this theory has held true 100% of the time. Although we've rarely had to replace a just-in-case item (fewer than five times for the two of us combined), we've never had to pay more than $20 or go more than 20 minutes out of our way to replace the item. This theory likely works 99% of the time for 99% of all items and 99% of all people. Including you.

More important, we haven't missed the hundreds of just-in-case items we've gotten rid of, and we didn't need to replace most of them.

Getting rid of these items clears one's mind, frees up their space, and takes the weight off his or her shoulders.

What are you holding on to *just in case*?

90/90 RULE

Rules can be arbitrary, restrictive, boring—but they are often helpful when we hope to make a change.

Whenever we attempt to simplify our lives, we often get stuck before we get started. When faced with a hoard of possessions—some useful, others not—it is difficult to determine what serves a purpose and what we're holding on to just in case, which makes letting go nearly impossible without some sort of rules to move us in the right direction.

Here's one that has worked for us: Look at a possession. Pick something. Anything. Have you used that items in the last 90 days? If you haven't, will you use it in the next 90? If not, then it's okay to let go.

Maybe your rule isn't 90 days. Maybe it's 120. Maybe it's six months. Whatever your rule, be honest with yourself. If your material possessions don't bring you joy, then they are likely in the way of a more intentional life.

WHEN EVERYTHING IS YOUR FAVORITE THING
by Joshua Fields Millburn

When you get rid of most of your stuff, your life invariably changes: Without all the things in your way, you have the opportunity to focus on the most important aspects of your life.

But there was also an unexpected benefit from my newly uncluttered life: Now I truly enjoy everything I own.

Before I embraced minimalism, I had a lot of stuff: A three bedroom house teeming with stuff. A basement and a two-car garage filled with boxes overflowing with stuff. Spare bedrooms and closets and cabinets jam-packed with stuff. Every nook, every cranny—more stuff.

It was hard to keep track of it, and all that stuff added very little value to my life. It often just made me feel anxious, overwhelmed, and depressed.

I was unhappy with the way I felt, so I started questioning everything I owned.

Today I don't own much, but the things I do own add immense value to my life. When I got rid of my extraneous material possessions, what remained were the things I use every day.

Now nearly everything I own is my *favorite* thing. All my clothes are my favorite clothes. All my furniture is my favorite furniture. All my possessions are my favorite possessions—all of which I enjoy every day of my life.

How about you? What if you enjoyed *everything* you owned? How would it make you feel if you were surrounded by your favorite things every day?

FAVORITE CLOTHES OF A MINIMALIST
by Joshua Fields Millburn

> *"Look at all those fancy clothes,*
> *but these gon keep us warm just like those."*
> —Jack Johnson

What does a minimalist wear? I'm surprised I get this question as often as I do—as if people expect to see me walking around in a loincloth—but, given the many misconceptions surrounding minimalism, I suppose it's a valid question.

My answer: a minimalist wears his or her favorite clothes every day. Most days I wear jeans, a teeshirt, and a pair of boots. Or, when I feel like it, I wear a crisp white button-up shirt, jeans, a blazer, colorful socks, and a clean pair of dress shoes. (I avoid logos because I don't enjoy being a walking billboard.)

I don't have many clothes now—and I still go to the Goodwill a few times a month to donate an item or two (if I'm not wearing it anymore, it gets donated)—but I thoroughly enjoy the clothes I own.

I don't, however, give sentimental meaning to my clothes. If all my clothes burned in a house fire tomorrow, it wouldn't be a big deal to me.

> *"What about those shoes you're in today?*
> *They'll do no good on the bridges*
> *you burnt along the way."*
>
> —Jack Johnson

SPILL BLEACH ON YOUR WARDROBE?
by Joshua Fields Millburn

What if you spilled bleach on half your wardrobe? What would you do?

Some hypothetical questions are so ridiculous we dismiss them as absurd, laughable queries. Sadly, though, the above question is *not* purely hypothetical.

After returning from the final leg of our recent tour, fatigued and murky-headed from cross-country traversing, I separated my dirty laundry into appropriate piles, prepping each color-coded assemblage for its usual rinse and spin cycles. Then, unknowingly and stupidly, I spilled a bottle of liquid bleach on literally half the clothes, staining the floor-strewn heaps, instantly ruining the majority of my wardrobe.

I was shocked by two things.

First, I was shocked by my brainlessness. How could I make such a ridiculous mistake? Truth be told, I simply wasn't paying attention. There's no other explanation. If there's a lesson to be learned here, it's that *attention must be paid*, even during the most mundane tasks.

Second, I was shocked I wasn't more horrified by my idiotic mistake. I should be outraged, right? Two years ago I would've been pissed; I would have fumed angrily and cursed the ceiling and hurled various breakable objects at one or more of my apartment's walls. But last week, as sodium hypochlorite soaked through my threads, I didn't react obnoxiously. Instead, I realized I couldn't control everything. I took a few deep breaths, snatched a mop from my closet, and started cleaning the mess I'd made. The sooner we clean up our mess, the sooner we can move on with life.

Sure, half my attire is ruined, but everything's fine. I'll replace some of the clothes if I need to, but my closet isn't upset, and nor should I be. Those clothes were just clothes —replaceable things that don't have any more meaning than the meaning I give to them. There's no case in crying over spilt milk—or, in this case—spilt bleach.

THINGS WE WALK AWAY FROM
by Joshua Fields Millburn

What are you prepared to walk away from? This oft-unasked question shapes one of the most important principles in my life.

We are all familiar with the age-old theoretical situation in which our home is burning and we must grab only the things that are most important to us. Of course, most of us would not dash into the inferno and reach for material things first—we'd ensure the safety of our loved ones and pets. Then, once they were safe, we'd grab only the irreplaceable things—photo albums, computer hard drives, family heirlooms. Everything else would be lost in the conflagration.

I tend to look at this situation a tad differently, though, taking the hypothetical a bit further.

There is a scene in *Heat* in which Neil McCauley (Robert De Niro) says, "Allow nothing in your life that you cannot walk out on in 30 seconds flat." Although my life isn't anything like McCauley's (he's the movie's bad guy), I share his sentiment. Almost everything I bring into my life—material possessions, ideas, habits, and even relationships—I must be able to walk away from at a moment's notice.

Many of you will disagree with me because this ideology might sound crass or insensitive, but I'd like to posit that it is actually the opposite: Our preparedness to walk away is the ultimate form of caring.

If I purchase new possessions, I need to make certain I

don't assign them too much meaning. Being able to walk away means I won't ever get too attached to my belongings, and being unattached to stuff makes our lives tremendously flexible—filled with opportunity.

If I take on a new idea or habit, I do so because it has the potential to add value to my life. New ideas shape the future Me. Same goes for new habits. Over time my ideas change, improve, and expand, and my current habits get replaced by new habits that continue to help me grow. Our readiness to walk away from ideas or habits means we're willing to grow—we're willing to constantly pursue a better version of ourselves.

If I bring a new relationship into my world, I know I must *earn* their love, respect, and kindness. I also expect they, too, are willing to walk away should I not provide the support and understanding they require. This means we must both work hard to contribute to the relationship. We must communicate and remain cognizant of each other's needs. And, above all, we must care. These fundaments— love, understanding, caring, communication—build trust, which builds stronger relationships in the long run. It sounds paradoxical, but our willingness to walk away actually strengthens our bond with others. And the opposite stance—being chained by obligation to a relationship—is disingenuous, a false loyalty birthed from pious placation.

There are obvious exceptions to this rule. There are certain things we cannot easily walk away from: a marriage, a business partnership, a job that pays the rent, a passion. The key is to have as few exceptions as possible.

Naturally, even these exceptions aren't exceptions for everyone. Marriages often end, as do businesses. People get laid off, and passions change over time. Even though we might not be able to walk away from these things in "30 seconds flat," we can ultimately walk away when these situations no longer add value to our lives (or worse, when they drain value from our lives).

Everything I allow into my life enters it deliberately. If my home was aflame, there's nothing I own that can't be replaced: All my photos are scanned. All my important files are backed up. And all my stuff has no real meaning. Similarly, I'm prepared to walk away from nearly anything—even our website, teaching, or writing—if need be. Doing so safeguards my continued growth and improves my relationships with others, both of which contribute to a fulfilling life, a life of meaning.

It was C.S. Lewis who, 50 years ago, eloquently said, "Don't let your happiness depend on something you may lose." In today's material world, a world of fear-fueled clinging, his words seem more apropos than ever.

HOME IS WHERE THE RED PHONE IS
by Joshua Fields Millburn

I don't enjoy traveling as much as some people.

Unless I'm touring, which I'm doing at the time of this writing and which I enjoy because the people are amazing, I tend to avoid exorbitant travel, opting instead to stay home in my community most of the time.

All my clothes would likely fit in a single suitcase, but I don't enjoy living out of a suitcase. I find value in traversing the globe, in discovering new cultures, in learning more about myself in the process—but I truly enjoy living in a home, a place I can call my own.

The problem with homes, however, is once we establish a long-term dwelling, it's easy to accumulate a bunch of junk we don't need.

I built my first house when I was 22—a feat that seems ridiculous now—but its size was even more ridiculous: It contained three bedrooms, even though only my former spouse and I lived there; it had a huge basement, which was a great place to hide last month's discarded new possessions (toys I no longer played with); it featured not only a gigantic living room but also an "entertainment room," which I think is pretty much just a fancy way to say "room with a too-large TV and expensive surround-sound system."

We think we have to fill all our space, every corner nook and hidden cranny crammed with supposed adornments. We believe if a room is nearly empty, then it is underutilized. So we buy stuff—silly stock paintings, decorative thingys, and IKEA furniture—to fill the void. What we're doing is attempting to establish the place in which we live as *our* home, an extension of ourselves. And so the logic goes: The more I buy, the more this place is my home.

The problem with this line of thinking is it's circuitous. Your home is your home for one reason: You call it your home. The stuff doesn't make it your home—*you* do.

If you need a reminder, you can do what I do: Find *one* thing, something unique, and display it somewhere prominent. For me, it's a red phone—a relic from my twelve years in the telecom industry. It's a simple, beautiful design that stands out (the same phone is in the Museum of Modern Art), and whenever I see it, I know I'm home. For you, your red phone could be a one-of-a-kind painting, a photograph, a child's framed drawing. When you have a single reminder of home, everything else begins to look superfluous, even silly.

What is your red phone?

I DON'T LOVE YOU ANYMORE
by Joshua Fields Millburn

There weren't any tears during my most recent breakup. No possessions strewn across the lawn. No passive aggression. No yelling, fighting, or angry text messages. There was only a twinge of relief—an unexpected pang of freedom.

The moment it all ended, I just stood there, an awkward silence between us. When I finally handed her the bag of clothes, I knew there was no turning back. But her features held no sign of sadness—more like a look of gratitude. As I drove away, I didn't once look in the rearview.

Thankfully this estrangement wasn't with a person, but with a large chunk of my wardrobe. If I would've anthropomorphized that bag of clothes before I handed it to the pretty girl at Goodwill, I would've told it, "It's not *you*—hell, it's not even *me*—it's *us*. We're no longer right for each other. I just don't love you anymore."

I realized it was time for us to part ways just last week, after I pulled on a teeshirt and immediately wanted to wear something else. It was a decent shirt, one I got a lot of use out of, but I didn't love wearing it anymore, and I hadn't loved wearing it in a while.

So I decided to go through my already minimal closet and dump every item I didn't love. I'd rather own just a few outfits—outfits I enjoy wearing, clothes I feel confident in, a wardrobe that brings me joy—than a mediocre collection of once-loved threads.

Sometimes love sunders, and we must move on. The things we once loved, we may not love forever.

A ROLEX WON'T GIVE YOU MORE TIME
by Joshua Fields Millburn

A friend recently emailed me to communicate the buyer's remorse he was experiencing after purchasing an expensive watch. Even though he's a successful entrepreneur who can afford to drop $10,000 on shiny wrist-ornamentation, he expressed pangs of post-purchase grief, sorrow, and regret.

He wasn't entirely sure why he felt this way, so he emailed me for advice. This is how I responded:

I know where you're coming from—as a guy who has owned several expensive watches (I owned more than one fancy watch during my lotus-eating twenties, although I don't own one now), I understand the allure. I could, of course, recite a dozen platitudes here—*an expensive watch can't give you more time, a puppet who enjoys his strings still isn't free, you are not the sum of your material possessions, our possessions possess us, etc.*—but it comes down to two things: Value and Quality of Life.

In terms of Value, does the watch actually add value to your life, or does it drain value? I'm not talking about monetary value (price is an arbitrary measurement), I'm talking real, intrinsic value. Is that watch worth $10,000 of your freedom? Is it worth the emotional stress you're going through while thinking about it?

I know these questions sound rhetorical, but they're not. I'm currently wearing a $100 pair of jeans, and, yes, they are worth $100 of my freedom to me. They are also my only pair of jeans, therefore I get immense value from them since I wear them almost every day. Does the watch do the same for you? If so, wear it with pride. If it doesn't, then ask yourself why you still own it—not why you bought it, but why you still own it. Is it a status thing? Is it part of your identity? Is it just an expensive personal logo?

At this point, the purchase is over—you needn't beat yourself up over it because you can't change it. It's a sunk cost, but you can change what you do going forward if you're not getting value from the purchase. If you get value from the watch—if it truly enhances your life—then why not keep it?

And when it comes to Quality of Life, you need to consider how the watch adds to the quality of *your* life. I earned about $200,000 a year at the peak of my corporate days, but I was miserable. My Quality of Life was poor.

Last year, however, at age 31, I made $27,000, which is actually less than I earned at eighteen. But with that $27,000 I still saved more than I've ever saved, paid off the rest of my debt, traveled more than I've ever traveled, and experienced life—real life—more than ever before. Though I make a multiplicity of millions less than the corporate big wigs I once aspired to be, and though I bring home roughly one-eighth of what I used to bring home at my pinnacle, I have an appreciably higher Quality of Life than most CEOs and my former self. Very few material possessions could enhance that Quality of Life; in fact, most would take away from it.

I obviously cannot and will not tell you what to do with your shiny timepiece. What I can tell you is I'm much happier without my expensive watches. Who needs to know the time all the time anyway?

I GOT RID OF 2,000 BOOKS
by Joshua Fields Millburn

I used to own 2,000 books. Slightly more than that, actually. I had all kinds of books: hard covers, paperbacks, trade paperbacks, literary fiction, writing and grammar books, books of photography, self-help books, my deceased father's collection of old medical journals, genre fiction, those cute little pop-up books—you name it.

I had shelves and shelves and more shelves of books, some

of which I'd actually read, and many of which I'd read *someday*—you know, whenever I got around to it.

Who was I kidding?

I thought my overflowing shelves of books made me look important, intelligent, and cool.

Look at me, I know how to read—a lot!

What's worse, I thought these books made me somebody. They were a part of my identity: Those books were a part of me. And once something's a part of your identity—once it becomes a part of *you*—it's exceedingly hard to shed.

This is true for anything we incorporate into our identities— our careers, our cars, our homes, our possessions, our sentimental items. These things become part of us, and they become anchors in our lives—anchors that keep us at bay, away from the freedom of the open seas.

Ironically, three quotes from a particular book I owned— Chuck Palahniuk's *Fight Club*—are what inspired me to get rid of the vast majority of my books a little over a year ago:

"Reject the basic assumptions of civilization, especially the importance of material possessions."

"The things you own end up owning you."

"It's only after we've lost everything that we're free to do anything."

These words resonated with me deeply: I could feel on my

nerve-endings what Palahniuk was saying. I read those quotes several times, and within a week sold or donated 98% of my books. I purchased a Kindle and kept one shelf of my favorite physical books. Some older books aren't yet on Kindle, which is a shame. In those rare cases, I'll get the book elsewhere—a public library, a local independent bookstore, online—and when I'm finished reading it, I'll often donate it.

I no longer own piles of books, but I read more than before. I enjoy each book, taking them in slowly, absorbing the knowledge, processing the information, contemplating their lessons—but I needn't retain the physical book to get value from its words.

Think about it: How much value was I placing in all the books I owned? Obviously it was far more than their real value. The real value was in the words—in the action of reading—not in the physical books themselves.

LETTING GO OF YOUR DVD COLLECTION

Are you one of those people who collects DVDs, proudly displaying your stockpile on a wall, shelf, or special area designated for your dozens of favorite movies?

Have you thought about why you own all those DVDs? Do you really plan to rewatch the same movies three, four—or a dozen times?

Both of us had fairly sizable DVD collections before taking our journeys into minimalism. We wasted thousands of dollars on these collections, often purchasing movies we'd already seen. And then we allowed our extensive collections to collect dust. Or we'd occasionally re-watch a movie, living in the past, attempting to reconstruct an old moment instead of creating new ones.

But *collecting* is just *hoarding* with a prettier name. Don't believe us? Look it up. The Oxford American Writer's Thesaurus lists the following synonyms under the first definition of *collection*: HOARD, pile, heap, stockpile.

Yes, collecting things you don't need—things you don't get value from—is tantamount to hoarding.

The two of us still watch movies, but we watch new movies, creating new experiences in our lives; we strengthen our relationships by enjoying movies with friends; we grow by talking about those experiences after they happen, developing a better understanding of ourselves in the process.

Let go of that DVD collection (you can sell it and make some money), and stop watching the same things over and over. Live your life instead. There is an entire world out there, and there is so much value you can add to that world, so much you can contribute beyond yourself—we're certain of it.

Or, how about this: keep the movies that add value to your life. There's nothing wrong with an occasional rerun, a glance in the rearview—but then look forward, and let go of the rest.

MORE IS LESS?

Less is more. We all know this saying, first popularized by minimalist architect Ludwig Mies van der Rohe, which has been transformed into a platitude by advertisers, TV shows, and even corporate America as it right-sizes people out of their livelihoods ("We'll have to learn to do more with less around here."). But is less *really* more? And if so, is the opposite true? Is more actually less?

Questions like this may be more important than you think.

The two of us enjoy taking commonly accepted truisms and trite stock phrases and flipping them on their axes, exploring the obverse side of cliches and hackneyed phrases, shedding light on the opposite sides of supposed facts.

For example, what moniker does our culture often assign to a well-adjusted, ostensibly successful person? We often say that these people are *anchored* ("He is such an anchored person."). We heard this term frequently during our late twenties: we were regularly described as anchored people, and for the longest time we took this as a compliment.

Then we stopped taking it at face value and asked, "What is an anchor?"

That question led us to an important discovery about our lives: an anchor is the thing that keeps a ship at bay, planted in the harbor, stuck in one place, unable to explore the freedom of the sea. Perhaps we *were* anchored—we knew we weren't happy with our lives—

and perhaps being anchored wasn't necessarily a *good* thing.

In the course of time, we each identified our own personal anchors—circumstances keeping us from realizing real freedom—and found they were plentiful (Joshua catalogued 83 anchors; Ryan, 54). We discovered big anchors (debt, bad relationships, etc.) and small anchors (superfluous bills, material possessions, etc.) and in time we eliminated the vast majority of those anchors, one by one, documenting our experience in our first book, *Minimalism: Live a Meaningful Life*.

It turned out being anchored was a terrible thing: it kept us from leading the lives we wanted to lead. Not all our anchors were bad, but the vast majority prevented us from encountering lasting contentment.

Are you an anchored person? Is that a good thing? What are some of your anchors? And what other axioms might you want to question?

Which brings us back to our original set of questions: Is less really more? If so, is more actually less?

We suggest the answer to both is *yes*.

Owning less stuff, focusing on fewer tasks, and having less in the way has given us more time, more freedom, and more meaning in our lives. Working less allows us to contribute more, grow more, and pursue our passions much more.

Having more time causes less frustration and less stress, more freedom adds less anxiety and less worry, and more meaning in our lives allows us to focus far less on life's excess in favor of what's truly important.

So, more is less? Yes, more or less.

CHAPTER THREE || **Technology**

A MINIMALIST APPROACH TO TECHNOLOGY

Our tools are only as good (or bad) as the person using them.

A chainsaw can cut down a rotting backyard tree, preventing it from impaling a neighbor's house—or that same chainsaw can be used to hurt our neighbor, to chop him into tiny pieces.

A can of paint can be used to beautify a home's facade—or neighborhood miscreants can use it to graffiti the walls at an otherwise pristine public park.

The same goes for technology. We can use Twitter, Pinterest, and Google+ to enrich our lives and the lives of others, to communicate and share in ways we've never been able to communicate before—or we can get stuck in social media's Bermuda Triangle, careening from Facebook to Instagram to YouTube, lost in the meaningless glow of our screens.

We can use our smartphones to photograph gorgeous landscapes, message loved ones, or map out directions to a distant national park (or—gasp!—to make phone calls)—or we can use that same device to Twitch: to incessantly check email, thumb through an endless stream of status updates, post vapid selfies, or partake in any other number of non-value-adding activities, all while ignoring the beautiful world around us.

It is up to us to determine how we use our chainsaws, paint cans, and technology. Our tools are merely tools, and it is our responsibility to ask important questions about how and why we use them. To become a Luddite is to avoid an entire world of possibilities, a better world that's enriched by the tools of technology. If used intentionally, we can change the world with these tools—or we can do a lot of harm. It's an individual choice: the world is literally at our fingertips, and it's up to us to act accordingly.

DIGITAL CLUTTER IS DIFFERENT

Digital clutter isn't nearly as problematic as physical clutter. Don't think so? Try to move 2,000 books to a new residence.

First, box up the physical books, taking them off their shelves one by one, labeling each box with its appropriate label (Self-help, Literary Fiction, Cambodian Interpretive Dance, etc.); then carry them to your vehicle, box by box, being careful not to drop them; and then haul them to your new home, carry them inside, carefully unpack each box, and re-shelve each individual book until every last book is (sort of) back where it was before you started this whole tedious exercise.

Then, next time you move, instead of boxing up all those books, grab your Kindle with all 2,000 titles, toss it into your bag, and be on your merry way.

It's not hard to realize which method is easier. We've done both. Joshua threw his back out (literally) while going through the first exercise. Shockingly, the Kindle exercise didn't have the same savage effect on his lumbar musculature.

That said, digital clutter can still be a significant problem. At *The Minimalists*, we advocate digitizing your physical items whenever you can, especially those old CDs, DVDs, photos, and files of paperwork you hardly ever need.

Getting these items out of the way is a monumental first step, but we also recommend constantly paring down your digital "stuff" as well. It's important to keep your email inbox, your files, your music, and your collection of recently downloaded cute cat videos organized to save you time.

It's equally important to get rid of files you no longer need. The rule of thumb we use is "the last six months." That is, if we haven't needed something in the last six months— saved documents, old college papers, Ryan's "special" recipe for Rice Crispy Treats—then we get rid of it. We do this twice a year; it takes less than an hour each time we purge our files.

As with any rule, there are exceptions. For example, taxes should obviously be kept for seven years (or longer depending on where you live). But these exceptions are few and far between.

As for pictures, you needn't delete any photos: you can use them every day if you have a digital picture frame.

You might be addressing your physical clutter, which is great. But when's the last time you purged your digital clutter?

SHIFTING TO A CULTURE OF ACCESS

There is a *Tosh.0* episode in which a faux-outraged Daniel Tosh decides to burn thousands of books during a mock protest. He takes to the streets, gasoline and matches in hand, and, in the skit's anti-climactic zenith, he sets his Kindle aflame.

Sure, it was a silly gesture, but apropos in the context of today's techno-cultural landscape.

There was a time, not long ago, when if we wanted immediate access to a large number of movies, we had to own hundreds of DVDs. If we wanted the ability to listen to a particular song on cue, our shelves needed to overflow with compact discs. And if we wanted to look smart, we needed a home library teeming with the oeuvres of all the most notable names in literature.

Today, of course, we needn't own a single DVD, CD, or

print book to have access to essentially unlimited options. With the click of a button, we can view any movie ever made, listen to any song ever produced, or read any page that's ever been printed.

That's not to say there's anything inherently wrong with the physical artifacts themselves. It's just that, like the record albums of yesteryear, we are able to own less in the deliberate pursuit of experiencing more. Much like a hipster's impressive vinyl collection, a well-curated bookshelf holds significantly more meaning than, say, clinging to a random collection of paperbacks just in case we might read them someday in some substitute future. The same can be said for DVDs, CDs, and…what's next? (Let's not even mention all those forgotten VHS and cassette tapes collecting dust in the basement.)

These relics (movies, music, books) are only the beginning. Imagine all the possibilities we will unveil as we shift from a culture of ownership—a culture obsessed with personally owning every object we can get our hands on—to a culture of access in which every citizen has unlimited access to virtually everything virtually.

Most of us never owned private basketball courts, bowling alleys, or swimming pools as children, yet we had access to these activities by way of our local communities (YMCA, public schools, parks). Now, in today's culture, access trumps ownership more than ever. With the rapid expansion of our sharing economy (Uber, Airbnb, Freecycle), we're living in a world that's radically different from the world of our Industrial Age predecessors.

This is great news, but it doesn't mean we must eschew

personal ownership. The opposite is true: with access to the non-physical world at our fingertips, the material things we own become more intentional, more deliberate, more purposeful. It's a beautiful paradox.

Technology has made this possible. No longer must we hoard; rather, with fewer physical possessions but greater access to the things that matter most, we can worry less about consuming, and focus more on creating and experiencing.

DON'T UPGRADE

The newest, latest, greatest version of Product X is available today. It's *only* X dollars and it does all the cool things you never knew it could do. If you act now, Product X will change your life.

We know we don't need Product X to live a good life (even if we really, really want it). We know we don't have to buy the new iPhone when our old phone works just fine. We know we don't need a new car just because the old one isn't as shiny, just as we know we don't need the latest version of software, iPad, television, laptop, or gadget to make us happy.

Advertisers spend millions of dollars to create a sense of urgency to make us drool over their products, but we can refuse to play that game. We can turn down the noise. We can focus on *what we have* instead of what we don't have. We already have everything we need.

Sure, sometimes things break or wear out over time. And when that happens, we are left with at least three options:

Go without. This option is almost taboo in our culture. It seems radical to many people. *Why would I go without when I could just buy a new one?* Often this option is the best option, though. When we go without, it forces us to question our stuff, it forces us to discover whether or not we need it—and sometimes we discover life without it is actually better than before.

Repair it. Sometimes we can't necessarily *go without*. But, instead of running out and procuring Product X, we can attempt to repair the item first. You wouldn't buy a new car just because the brakes needed to be replaced, would you? The same goes for many other household items.

Replace it. As a last resort, we can replace things. But even when we do this, we can do so mindfully. We can purchase used items, we can buy products from local businesses, and often we can downgrade and still have what's necessary to live a fulfilling life.

REPROGRAMMING THE TWITCH
by Joshua Fields Millburn

Must one unplug from reality to properly observe reality?

Going without a phone for any extended period of time seems to be the modern-day equivalent of a vow of silence. Two months ago I decided to 86 my phone for 60 days as an experiment, just to see what would happen, just to see whether my world would keep spinning. People were shocked. Some were appalled. Some people were flat out worried about me.

I'll skip the overused Matrix references about unplugging from the grid and simply say I learned more about myself than I intended. I couldn't have done so without disconnecting for a while, without stepping back and actually thinking about my life in a deliberate, uninterrupted way.

This is what I learned during my two months of quiet time:

We have weird expectations. I realized I needed to get rid of my cellphone for a while when I felt pressure to respond to text messages, email, and social media throughout the day. We all have different expectations. You might expect someone to respond in an hour, someone else might expect a response in ten minutes, another person might expect it the same day. These expectations are arbitrary. When I eliminated my ability to immediately respond, I was able to toss everyone's expectations into the ether.

Meaningful conversations. Without the banality of ephemeral text conversations, my real face-to-face conversations have become more meaningful. When I'm spending time with my closest friends and loved ones, I now have more to discuss in earnest. I enjoy these conversations more than ever.

People are supportive and understanding. When we make changes in our lives, we're often afraid of what people will think. *Will they think I'm crazy, stupid, or out of* *touch?* People are more supportive and understanding than we think—particularly the people closest to us. Especially when we discuss our changes with them and let them know we're making the changes so we can live happier lives: our true friends want us to be happy.

We program ourselves. Without knowing it, our daily activities have a profound impact on our future selves. I used to reach for my BlackBerry every few minutes no matter where I was—even at the urinal. Even when the phone wasn't with me, I had programmed myself to reach for it. What an obscene Twitch.

We can reprogram ourselves. Similarly, we can change these patterns. When we remove a habit from our lives, we become acutely aware of how that habit affected our lives. This is true for any habit: smoking, over-eating, etc. It took 22 days for me to reprogram the Twitch, 22 days of pausing and noticing why I was Twitching. After 22 days I no longer felt the urge to immediately react; I no longer felt the need to pacify myself with transitory activities like texting or responding to emails during every moment of "downtime."

Downtime is a misnomer. We used to have precious interstitial zones in which we could find momentary solace: airports, checkout lines, waiting rooms, and other transient sanctuaries in which we could bask in reverie. No longer is this the case. Now, everyone seems to be on their phones during these fleeting moments. They are attempting to be more productive or interactive, but perhaps stopping and thinking is far more productive than fiddling with our phones.

The world goes on. Without a cellphone, without the Internet, without a TV, the world keeps turning. You can test anything for a short period of time to see whether it's right for you. It's not hard to give up anything when you live in the real world. There wasn't a single time when I actually *needed* my phone in the last two months. Sure, there were times when it was inconvenient, times when I had to fight through the frustration—but that was a small price to pay to reprogram the Twitch.

Yes, I'll go back to using a cellphone for practical purposes —GPS, necessary phone calls, the Dictionary app I missed dearly, a memo pad, and a few other useful apps—but I'll use it utterly differently going forward. I'm not going to use it to check email anymore, I'm not going to use it to send text messages while standing at a urinal, and I'm not going to rely on it as my primary means of interacting with the world around me. My cellphone usage will be more intentional than before. My phone will be a tool, not an appendage.

SLEEP, SEX, AND RERUNS
by Joshua Fields Millburn

As far as I'm concerned, a bed has two purposes—neither of which include watching latenight reruns.

Look around: we are in the throes of a torrent of multitasking. Everyone is attempting to "increase productivity" in their business and personal lives with their iPhones, iPads, iMacs, and iWhatevers. Multitasking is endemic to our culture.

We must accept that no matter how much we multitask, no matter how many concurrent emails, texts, and status updates we respond to, we'll never get *everything* done. That's because there's an infinite amount of tasks to undertake once you've "completed everything."

We are constantly bombarded by contemporaneous inputs, and thus it's more important than ever to find sanctuary in interstitial zones: waiting rooms, the grocery store, the bedroom.

So, I've taken back my bedroom. When in bed, I refuse to watch TV, surf the Web, or text message—I can do those things elsewhere, another time. I find refuge in knowing when my head hits the pillow, I'll either be sleeping or intimate with someone else, but nothing else.

There's comfort in singletasking.

CAN I GET HIM TO STOP WATCHING TV?

A reader, Michelle, wrote seeking our advice:

I am working on creating a minimalist lifestyle for my family, but I have hit a roadblock and hope you can help, especially from the male perspective. In our house we watch TV, always have. I despise the TV because my husband spends so much time watching sports, it's often used as a babysitter for our kids when I am not home, it costs us money (granted the cable doesn't cost that much), and most of all it sucks up our time! What, if any, suggestions do you have to get this time sucker out of my house without causing a war with my husband? He is embracing minimalism, at least in theory, because while we didn't have tons of stuff, we got rid of lots of junk and he likes the feeling of more space, but I mention his beloved TV and it's a whole different ballgame.

Our recommendations:

Start with yourself. Before you can convince anyone to change, you must first change yourself.

Reduce. How many TVs do you have? If it's more than one, reduce them by half initially. Get down to one TV over time.

Bedroom. Whatever you do, get the TV out of the bedroom. There are better ways to entertain each other in bed.

Schedule. Schedule your viewing. Don't watch television unless you have scheduled your viewing at least 24 hours in advance. Ask your husband to attempt this with you for ten days (an experiment of sorts).

Limit. Limit yourself to X hours per week. Track your viewing. Do this together for ten days.

Friends. Invite friends over to watch TV with you during your scheduled viewing, and then talk about what you watched afterward—this will strengthen your relationships.

Replace. Replace TV with other activities. Just getting rid of TV is boring—what else can you do together instead of watch television?

Once you do these things, your husband will likely follow. There's nothing wrong with owning a TV—it's when we spend too much time watching television that it has a negative effect on our lives.

CHECK EMAIL LIKE A MINIMALIST
by Joshua Fields Millburn

Most of us receive a multitude of emails each day. It's easy to address them one by one, filtering and sorting and replying to them as they tumble into our inboxes.

Most of the emails I receive are either positive or pointless—nice words from readers (positive) or junk mail I do my best to filter out (pointless). Thus, it's only logical to want to check my email frequently, receiving textual praise while clearing the clutter. It's a win-win, right? After all, who doesn't want constant positive feedback? And who doesn't want to *feel* productive?

This sounds ideal, except for one problem: we have real lives.

You see, living in our inboxes—something I did for a long time, especially during my twelve years in the corporate world—forces us to be on edge, always seeking the next nugget of digital applause, always anticipating the next question, the next "follow-up," the next "action item." Worse, it keeps me away from living a fulfilling life, one that doesn't revolve around the white glow of my computer screen.

The problem with email is it's never enough. Even when we whittle our incoming messages down to zero, we're constantly waiting for the next fleeting bit of good information. I call these bits "food pellets from the universe."

Similar to a lab rat, we have trained ourselves to click that "get mail" button to receive these food pellets. Hit the lever, get the food. Hit the lever, get the food. Hit the lever, get the food.

Sometimes the food is tasty—a kind message from a friend, a thoughtful question, a hilarious link from Nicodemus. But most of the time these food pellets are filled with empty calories and they taste like cardboard.

So instead of checking my email throughout each day, I check it once a day at most, and some days I don't check it at all.

A handful of changes in my life have made this shift possible—and far less stressful than you might think.

Home. I don't have Internet at home. This one change, albeit utterly frustrating at first, is likely the most productive thing I've ever done. Because I don't have Internet at home, it is impossible for emails to penetrate the walls of my abode.

Phone. I don't get emails on my phone. Once I brought my cellphone back into my life—after going two months without it—I discovered that it was better and far less stressful to remove email from it altogether. Now I use my phone to text and (ahem) talk.

Planning. When I check email, I do so deliberately. I set aside a block of time, clear my plate, and embrace the messages on *my* schedule, on *my* terms, when it's convenient for *me*. If I do it right, it's possible to enjoy myself, even when I'm checking my email.

Expectations. It's important to set the proper expectations with people. Let people know how you feel about email (they likely feel the same way). Ask them to respect your time and attention. My friends know I don't like receiving superfluous emails, and if they must send me an email, then I likely won't respond right away. My students know I don't respond the same day, either. When I do respond, it's thoughtful, succinct, and, above all, value-adding. The best question to ask yourself before clicking the send button is, *Does this email add value?*

DELETING MUSIC YOU NO LONGER LISTEN TO
by Joshua Fields Millburn

Are you actually going to listen to that Ricky Martin album again? Then why is it still on your iPod? Why do you keep music you haven't listened to in years? Do you keep it just in case?

I certainly used to.

Once upon a time, I owned more than 2,000 CDs. This is no surprise to people who know me well. I'm an auditory learner—which is the reason my writing often has a run-on-ish, out-loud, tumbling-words pace and cadence—and so music has played a significant role in shaping my life.

Because music was important to me—because it added immense value to my life—I transferred all my CDs (literally all 2,000 of them) one by one to my iTunes library, until my hard drive was bloated with more than 20,000 songs, from A-ha (hey, no laughing!) to ZZ Top and everything in-between.

Music is a special art form. It is different from movies, television, or even books. Music is created to be consumed more than once, absorbed over time, shaping itself to your consciousness after many listens. Movies and books are generally created to be consumed once (maybe twice), not repeatedly. That's why I advocate getting rid of old movies and old books.

But today, I'd also like you to consider getting rid of some of your music.

Recently, I deleted 80% of the music in my iTunes library. How did I select what to delete? I spent a few hours shuffling through my albums, starting at the top (yes, if you're wondering, A-ha was the first to go). I deleted everything I hadn't listened to in the last six months. Billy Joel: gone. Guns N' Roses: gone. Corey Hart: mostly gone—"Sunglasses at Night" survived the cut.

All that's left is the good stuff—the music I enjoy listening to. Now, my iTunes library is easier to navigate, it's clutterfree, and it's filled with music I love: The National, David Gray, Talib Kweli, et al.

How much of your music is in the way of the good stuff?

ONLINE CONGRUENCY

by Joshua Fields Millburn

I'm sitting in a diner in Birmingham, Alabama, smelling the ground coffee beans wafting through the air, sifting through emails from friends. One in particular stands out.

A close friend is amid the tedious med-school application process, and she's worried about her Facebook account being used against her by the folks who review applications. Now, I don't even have an undergraduate degree, so I'm likely an unfit advisor on grad-school matters, but then again I don't really see this as a collegiate affair at all. Rather, it's a matter of congruency.

For the longest time, I myself led two separate lives: professional JFM and personal JFM. There was Corporate Me, prim and proper, ostensibly flawless; and then there was Creative Me, flawed but beautiful (beautiful because of the flaws, perhaps). For obvious reasons, the two mixed about as well as glass rubbing against concrete. So I kept them segregated. Corporate Me didn't talk about his love for writing, and Creative Me loathed hiding himself from the world. It was almost as though both sides were ashamed of each other.

Over time this took its toll, until eventually I realized living two separate lives was exhausting, even disingenuous. So instead of hiding one half from the other, I decided to change my activity to align both halves.

In my friend's case, she wanted to go as far as changing her name on social media. My advice: Do you do anything online you're not proud of in real life? If so, I wouldn't change my name—I'd change my online activity. Your online persona should be a mirror of you, and nothing to be ashamed of.

For me, there isn't an online self and a real-life self these days—just *myself*. Whether I write something online, speak to a crowd of people, or have a one-on-one conversation with a friend, my life is congruent.

Don't get me wrong: I still have a private life. Like most people, I enjoy having sex, sending tarty text messages, and walking around the house naked—I just don't share those details publicly. Not because I'm ashamed, but because they are private (and because they don't contribute to the greater good). There's a big difference between a public online profile (an extension of one's self) and a private intimate conversation (personal interactions not meant for public consumption).

Deciding what's private and what's public is a personal matter. Share whatever you'd like. Just don't be ashamed of who you are. Shame is ugly, and you're far too beautiful for that.

CHAPTER FOUR || **Finances**

A MINIMALIST'S THOUGHTS ON MONEY

by Joshua Fields Millburn

I don't think about money the way I used to.

I used to think money was more important than just about everything else in life. So I sacrificed to make money, and then I sacrificed more to make more, and then I sacrificed even more to make even more, working too many hours, forsaking my health, forsaking the people closest to me, forsaking everything important in pursuit of the almighty dollar.

The more things I forsook, the more important the money became. Something was missing.

> *"I'm dizzy from the shopping mall*
> *I searched for joy, but I bought it all*
> *It doesn't help the hunger pains*
> *and a thirst I'd have to drown first to ever satiate"*
> —John Mayer, "Something's Missing"

I made good money—great money—during my days in the corporate arena, but the problem was I spent even better money. And that was a serious source of dissatisfaction in my life, one that would haunt me for most of my twenties.

When I was nineteen, I worked six or seven days a week, and I earned more than $50,000 a year, which for a degree-less poor kid from Dayton, Ohio, that's a lot of money—more money than my mother ever earned. The problem was that when I was earning 50 grand, I was spending 65; and then when I was earning 65, I was spending 80. Eventually, I'd worked my way up the corporate ladder, working 362 days a year (literally), and I was earning a six-figure salary. That sounds great, but I was still spending more than I was bringing home, and that equation never balances.

So instead of bringing home a great salary, I brought home debt, anxiety, and overwhelming amounts of discontent. My love and hatred of money (love of spending it, hatred of never having enough) was, in fact, my largest source of discontent.

Call me stupid. Go ahead, you should. I *was* stupid. I wasn't stupid just because I was wasting my income, though—I was far more stupid because of the value I gave to money. I told myself I was a number, there was a dollar sign on my head, I could be bought. I told others they could take my time and my freedom in exchange for green pieces of paper with dead slave owners' faces printed on them.

That changed when I stopped giving such importance to money. I need money to pay rent, to put food on the table, to put gas in the car, to pay for health insurance—but I needn't struggle to earn money to buy crap I don't need.

Minimalism has allowed me to get rid of life's excess so I can focus on what's essential. And now, at 31, I make less money than my ignorant nineteen-year-old self, and yet I'm not in debt, I'm not struggling, and most important, I'm happy.

Now, before I spend money, I ask myself one question: *Is this worth my freedom?*

Is this coffee worth $2 of my freedom?
Is this shirt worth $30 of my freedom?
Is this car worth $20,000 of my freedom?

In other words, am I going to get more value from the thing I'm about to purchase, or am I going to get more value from my freedom?

Don't you think it's a question worth asking yourself?

These days, I know every dollar I spend adds immense value to my life. There is a roof over my head at night, the books or the music I purchase bring me joy, the few clothes I own keep me warm, the experiences I share with others at a movie or a concert add value to my life and theirs, and a cup of tea with my best friend becomes far more significant than a trip to the mall ever could.

I no longer waste my money, and thus it's far less important to pursue it endlessly.

MONEY AND POVERTY DON'T BUY HAPPINESS

People have strange conceptions about money. When we don't have it, we believe money will make us happier. When we do have money, however, we tend to want more.

The odd thing is, we all know—at least intellectually—money won't buy happiness. Unfortunately, we've been steeped in a culture so heavily mediated we've started believing the lies. The cars, the houses, the stuff—living the so-called Dream will make us happy. This is not true, of course.

The opposite, however, is also *not* true. A life of poverty—a life of perpetual deprivation—isn't joyous either.

You see, there's nothing inherently wrong with money, just as there's nothing innately wrong with material possessions or working a 9-to-5. We all need some stuff, and we all have to pay the bills. It's when we put money and possessions first, and we lose sight of our real priorities. When we lose sight of life's purpose.

Maybe getting some of the excess stuff out of the way—clearing the clutter from our lives—can help us all save money and make room for the most important things in life: health, relationships, growth, contribution, community. Money helps accentuate these areas, but the size of your wallet is much less important once your priorities are in line with your beliefs.

MONEY DOES NOT BUY BETTER HABITS
by Joshua Fields Millburn

I'm not averse to earning money—that would be silly. I am, however, much more concerned with outcome than income.

A common mistake we make is we often assign money as our primary driver of happiness: *If I make $X, then I'll be happy.*

Once this happens, though—once we earn $X—we quickly discover the equation is broken. There is, after all, a reason most lottery winners end up broke: bad habits. Besides, there are plenty of miserable millionaires and countless happy poor folks.

A much better conductor of individual contentment, then, has little to do with money: our daily habits. The outcome of better habits is more rewarding than your income will ever be.

We have a much better chance of radically improving our happiness by just changing our habits—by forming new, empowering daily rituals—and we needn't earn exorbitant amounts of cash to do so.

High income or no, we must simply avoid passivity in favor of active, engaged, deliberate tasks. We must acknowledge our mistakes, make the right direction-changing decisions, and then take incremental actions each day. Over time, as we move farther in the right direction, we'll be able to wave at our bad habits in the rearview, happy and content, driving toward a more worthwhile horizon.

This is all, of course, not as easy as it sounds—but it's simpler than you may think.

STIMULATE THE ECONOMY LIKE A MINIMALIST

If everyone immediately stopped spending their money, our economy would crash. This goes without saying. Consequently, one of the most prominent (supposed) arguments many people have against minimalism is that if everyone became a minimalist, then we'd all be doomed: the financial system as it stands today would collapse, and we would no longer have the wealth necessary to purchase cheap plastic shit from Walmart.

There are several problems with this point of view, some obvious, some a bit more obscure.

First, no informed person would argue that we should stop spending money or that we must stop consuming. Consumption is not the problem—*consumerism* is.

Consumerism is compulsory, insipid, impulsive, unfocused, misguided. Worst of all, it is seductive: consumerism's shiny facade promises more than it can possibly deliver, because love, happiness, contentment, and satisfaction are all internal feelings that cannot be commodified, and the truth is that once our basic needs are met, the acquisition of trinkets does little for our lifelong well-being.

Using consumerism to stimulate the economy is like fixing a cracked mirror with a hammer: it only worsens the problem. Yes, trade is an important part of any society. Circumventing consumerism, however, doesn't imply that minimalists sidestep commerce; rather, minimalism is predicated on intentionality, which means we spend our money more deliberately.

Minimalists invest in experiences over possessions. Travel, indie concerts, vacations, community theater, etc.: we can all spend money without acquiring new material things.

Minimalists buy new possessions carefully. To do so we must ask better questions, like, *Will this good or service add value to my life?*

Minimalists support local businesses. Local, indie shops tend to be less motivated by profit. Sure, they need to make money to keep the lights on—and there's nothing wrong with that—but earning a buck usually isn't the primary concern of the local bookstore, restaurant, or bike shop. They are in business because they are passionate about their product or service, and they want to share that passion with their patrons. Passion begets greater quality and better service, which makes the money they earn well-deserved.

Ultimately, minimalists aren't interested in "stimulating" the economy—stimulation is short-lived. We'd rather improve our economy's long-term health by making better individual decisions about consumption, getting involved in our community, and supporting local businesses who care. If more people do this, we'll build a stronger economy, one that's predicated on personal responsibility and community interaction, not a false sense of urgency and the mindless stockpiling of junk we never needed in the first place.

FOOL PRICE
by Joshua Fields Millburn

I had to purchase a new pair of bluejeans recently. They are the only jeans I own. My previous pair, tattered after two years of literal wear and tear, were beyond repair. Soon, the boots I've been wearing since age 29, now sole-less and scuffed from twelve seasons of use, will need to be replaced. I plan on ordering a new pair this week.

The bluejeans were $100, the boots $300. Full Price, both of them.

You see, I avoid Sale Price whenever I can, opting instead to pay Full Price. Plus, even though I don't earn a lot of money, I tend to purchase higher quality items, not for their brand names, but because I'm willing to pay more for things that look good, work well, and last longer.

Because I'm responsible with money, the higher priced, higher quality items actually cost less in the long run—I use them till they're finished. (I wore my jeans roughly 700 times, my boots 1,000; therefore, I paid only 14¢ every time I pulled on my pants, 30¢ each time I stepped into my shoes.)

The reason I avoid Sale Price, though, has less to do with quality or money and more to do with my own impulses. I prefer to pay Full Price because it makes me question the purchase a great deal. When I discover something I want to buy, I must think it over and spend time budgeting for it, all the while questioning whether the new possession will add real value to my life.

Conversely, Sale Price is the compulsory price—a fool's price.

Not long ago, I played the fool. Repeatedly. I fell for all the tropes of Sale Price: *Act now! Limited time only! While supplies last!* But much like Pavlov's bell, these clever stratagems incite a false sense of scarcity that clouds our perception of reality, prodding us to act on impulse. Sure, you might save 70% off that clearance-rack dress you sort of like, but you'll save 100% if you just leave the store without it.

When I pay Full Price I know my purchase is well thought-out, more deliberate. Don't get me wrong, though: if the jeans or boots would've been less expensive, I still would've purchased them—if I *needed* them, but not because they were on sale.

NEED, WANT, LIKE

Maybe you're dying to do something different with your life. Maybe you want to discover your mission, change careers, or take a midlife sabbatical, but it doesn't seem sensible to make a big change, to do something different, does it? You're tied to your soul-crushing job, fettered to an income you've become accustomed to—it has a stranglehold on your life.

But you can break free of the shackles of unnecessary obligation and its laundry list of side effects: stress, debt, discontent, anxiety, depression. The two of us took back control of our lives with a simple, three-category list. You can do likewise.

First, write down all your expenses—every last dollar you spend. Mortgage, car payment, rent, credit card statements, meals, gasoline, electricity, student loans, bottled water, trips to Starbucks, retirement, healthcare, savings, etc. Write it all down. *All of it!* Now separate those expenses into three categories.

Category One: *Needs*. What do you really, truly need to live? Everyone is different, but most of us have the same basic Needs. What do *you* need? Food? Shelter? Super Nintendo?

Category Two: *Wants*. This category is important. Many of the things you want can lead to happiness. The problem is we indulge too many of our Wants—new vehicles, designer clothes, impulse buys—many of which end up being Likes instead of Wants. Another way to look at this category is to ask yourself, *What adds value to my life?*

Category Three: *Likes*. This category is for when you say things like, "Yeah, I like my satellite radio, but I don't get a ton of value from it." Or, "I like that dress, it's *soooo* my style, but I don't really need any new clothes." Many of the things we just sort of *like* suck up a ton of our income, and it's hard to notice during our consumer-driven frenzies. These Likes are often impulse purchases that feel great in the moment, but the post-purchase methamphetaminic high wears off by the time the credit card statement enters your mailbox. It's an odd double-bind: it turns out you don't really *like* many of your Likes at all.

You've made your list, you've got your three categories, and now it's time to take action. We'll start from the bottom and work our way up. (This is what we did before we were ready to make any big life changes.)

Month 1, get rid of 100% of your Likes. All of them—gone.

Month 2, get rid of 100% of your Wants. Yes, all of them (at first). Once you're headed down the right path, and you've made the necessary changes in your life, you can reintroduce your Wants one at a time, though you'll likely realize you want far fewer of your old Wants (your pacifiers) once you're traversing a more meaningful path. Remember, your Wants are important—they add value to your life—but they're not more important than changing your life.

Month 3, reduce your Needs by at least 50%. More if you can. You might be thinking, *But I need a roof over my head! I need to eat! I need my MTV!* Okay, you needn't get rid of everything: you needn't live in a hut and eat only Ramen noodles. But you can significantly reduce your cost of living. Can you sell your home like both of us did? Can you cut your rent by 50% (or by 75% like we did)? Can you sell your car and get a cheaper one like Ryan? Can you find ways to reduce your food costs by 50% like Joshua? Of course you can. While there isn't a cookiecutter answer for anyone, you can reduce your expenses and live more deliberately. *This* is the high price of pursuing your dreams. Unfortunately, many people aren't willing to pay the price, and so their dreams never become Musts for them—they remain Shoulds, which eventually turn into Wishes, which one day become Never Going to Happens—and that story always has a sad ending.

But once you remove yourself from the clutches of money, you'll worry less; and once you get rid of your worries, you'll have nothing to worry about—you'll be able to make any change you want to make.

That doesn't mean you should go out and quit your job today—it means you should plan accordingly, and when you're ready, you can make the right decision. Knowing you're no longer trapped by the trappings of your previous income requirements, you can make a *real* decision, one that's not based on fear.

Every beautiful change takes time and action: it takes time for a flower to bloom. These changes are scary at first (they were terrifying for us). And although big changes are often simple, they're rarely easy—but nothing worth doing is ever easy.

FINANCIAL FREEDOM

Money: it tears families apart, ruins marriages, and keeps people from pursuing their dreams. Money troubles inject unnecessary stress, anxiety, and arguments into our daily lives, which keeps us in perpetual discontent. We never seem to have enough, and, living paycheck to paycheck, we can't ever get ahead.

But it doesn't have to be this way.

We—Joshua & Ryan—know first hand. The road to financial freedom was a long trek for each of us. Even though we had prestigious six-figure careers, we struggled with money back then; we weren't financially free for a long time. It wasn't until we walked away from those careers (after devising a plan, of course) that we discovered how to get out of debt, how to eliminate unnecessary expenses, how to plan for our future, how to master our finances.

While we all need to make money to live—and there's certainly nothing wrong with earning a great salary—taking control of your financial life involves much more than adjusting your income upward: it involves making repeated good decisions with the resources you have, changing your financial habits, and living deliberately. None of which is inherently *easy*—especially under the tyranny of today's instant-gratification culture—but fortunately, regaining control of your finances is *simple*.

A few years ago, overwhelmed by money's rapacious tug on our lives, the two of us decided to change: we decided to take back control of our finances and our lives. These are the five steps we took, and they are the same principles we use today to ensure we'll never again struggle with money.

1. **BUDGET**. Most of us have no idea where our money is going: we think we know, but we don't really know. This is doubly true for those of us who are married or live with a significant other. So, the first step toward financial freedom is establishing a written monthly budget. Note the three key words here: written, monthly, and budget.

A few guidelines:

Categories. Identify what's truly necessary by identifying all of your monthly expenses based on the past six months, and then divide your expenses into three categories, as outlined in the preceding essay, "Need, Want, Like." Write down *every* expense (food, housing, utilities, insurance, cars, gas, transportation, clothes, credit cards, phones, Internet, pets, entertainment, etc.); triple-check the list with your significant other or a friend; and then use your Need, Want, Like categories to prioritize and cut wherever you can. The stricter you are, the sooner you'll be free.

Boundaries. Give every dollar a destination at the beginning of the month. By establishing these boundaries, you won't worry about what you can and can't purchase because money that wasn't assigned at the beginning of the month can't be spent mid-month.

Teamwork. Everyone in your household—even your children—must have a say in the written budget. This is the only way to get every person's buy-in. Working together means taking from one category to fund another (e.g., extracting money from, say, your clothing budget to fund your entertainment budget) until each person is on the same page. Once everybody is on board—once everyone is committed to financial freedom—it is much easier to gain the traction you need.

Adjust. You'll have some slip-ups along the way—that's all right, it's part of the process. At first, you and your family should scrutinize your written budget daily—and, eventually, weekly—adjusting accordingly until your whole family is comfortable with your set monthly allocations. The first month is the most difficult, but by the third month you'll curse yourself for wasting so much money during your budget-less days.

Safety. Shit happens, so it's best to create a Safety Net savings account with $500–$1000 for emergencies. Now listen: do *not* touch this money unless there is a true emergency (car repairs, medical bills, job loss, etc.). Your Safety Net will allow you to stay on budget even when life punches you in the face. Over time, once you're out of debt (step three below), your Safety Net will grow to include several months of income. But for now, worry only about the first $500–$1000 to start, which you'll want to keep in a separate Safety Net account to avoid temptation.

2. **PAY YOURSELF (INVEST)**. Most of us hear the word *invest* and we panic. Investing seems so complicated, so abstract, so not-something-I-can-wrap-my-head-around. Instead of thinking of it as *investing money*, think of it as *paying your future self*. And with today's online tools, you needn't be overwhelmed—investing is easier than ever. Anyone can (and must) do it.

As for Joshua & Ryan, we both use a simple online-investment tool as our personal savings, planning, and investing software. We invest our money into four separate buckets using an online software: Safety Net, Retirement Fund, House Fund, and Wealth-Building Fund (visit TheMinimalists.com/freedom to learn more about our specific investment strategy, as well as some free tools we use to keep us on track).

Right now is the best time to start planning for your future. Whether you're planning for retirement, wanting to start a business, saving for a home, building a larger Safety Net, or focusing on long-term wealth-building, *now* is the best time to begin. Not next week, not even tomorrow, *today*. Even if you have no money to invest, you *must* devise a plan to begin investing in your future self. The best way to do this is to automate your investments, which takes the guesswork out of investing. The future won't wait. Do it today. Even if that means 1% of your income, or even $20 a month, to start. Your future self will thank you.

3. **DEBT-FREE**. Contrary to what some academics might tell you, there is no such thing as "good debt." Let's say that again (read it out loud): THERE IS NO SUCH THING AS GOOD DEBT. Some debt is worse than other debt, but it's never "good."

You will not feel free until you are debt-free. The debtor is always slave to the lender. Besides, it feels amazing to have no car payments, no credit-card payments, and no student-loan payments looming in the shadows of your lifestyle.

Throughout our twenties we both had excessive piles of debt—more than six-figures each. It was a debilitating feeling—a complete loss of freedom.

Although there are no magic bullets, the strategy we've seen work best is Dave Ramsey's book, *Total Money Makeover*, a detailed, step-by-step formula that both of us used to create a detailed plan, cut up our credit cards, and face our debts head-on. (You can also read Joshua's debt-free story at TheMinimalists.com/debt.)

4. **MINIMIZE**. Of course minimalism was a key component in our own journeys toward financial freedom. By clearing

the clutter from our lives, we were able to focus on eliminating debt, changing our habits, and making better decisions with fewer resources.

We also learned that by simplifying—by identifying which material possessions weren't adding value to our lives—we were able to more quickly become debt-free by selling more than *half* our stuff locally (yard sales, consignment shops, flea markets) and online (eBay, Craigslist, Autotrader).

No, minimalism is *not* about deprivation—we don't want anyone to "live without" in the name of minimalism—but sometimes it makes sense to temporarily deprive ourselves of temporary satisfactions when we are attempting to move our lives in a better direction.

For example, as we were tackling our debts, Joshua sold his oversized house and moved into a tiny apartment. Ryan sold his fancy new car and purchased a decade-old vehicle without a monthly payment. We both jettisoned our cable subscriptions, satellite radio, and other luxury bills, which saved us hundreds of dollars each month. We also did "strange" things like deliver pizzas, work overtime, and find other ways to supplement our income in the short-term so we could pay off our debts faster. Plus, we sold hundreds of items—electronics, furniture, clothes, DVDs, books, collectibles, tools, yard equipment—that weren't essential, and we used that money to further pay down our debts. Anything that wasn't nailed to the floor found its way to eBay. Now everything we own serves a purpose or brings us joy, and we don't miss any of the trinkets of yesteryear.

Don't know how to start minimizing? Visit our Start Here

page at TheMinimalists.com/start for tips and best practices.

5. **CONTRIBUTE**. The shortest path toward freedom is appreciating what you already have. One of the best ways to find gratitude for the gifts you've already been given is to change your perspective.

To do so, donate your most precious asset: your time. Bring your family to a local soup kitchen, foodbank, or homeless shelter. Tutor less-privileged children in your city. Help the elderly with groceries or in-home care. Work on low-income houses with Habitat for Humanity. There are more resources than ever to help you contribute beyond yourself—just do an Internet search for volunteer opportunities in your area.

Whatever you do to build your contribution muscle, it needn't be grandiose—it need only contribute to someone else's life. If you do this for a few weeks, you'll realize your financial problems are tiny compared to many of the problems in the world around you. By discovering the smallness of your financial woes, you'll feel empowered to take massive action and beat the crap out of your relatively miniature problems.

In a short period of time—two or three years—your entire life can radically transform from what it is today. All it takes is a plan (which you now have), determination (i.e., turning your *shoulds* into *musts*), and consistent action in the right direction.

CONCLUSION: SIMPLE AIN'T EASY. Financial freedom isn't easy, but you knew that before reading this essay. The exciting part about these five principles is they apply to anyone, anywhere on the socioeconomic ladder. Whether you earn minimum wage or six-figures, whether you are single or have half-a-dozen children, we have seen these principles work for thousands of people—because it's not about our income level; it's about the decisions we make with the resources we have.

You are now equipped with a recipe to make outstanding financial changes. You are obviously welcome to add your own ingredients to taste, but when it comes to true financial freedom, these five ingredients—budget, invest, eliminate debt, minimize, contribute—are nonnegotiable. All five are necessary.

Yes, you still have a considerable amount of research and planning and hard work ahead of you—but most important, you have to take action today. Diligence is paramount.

11 SIGNS YOU MIGHT BE BROKE

You might be broke if:

1. **You're living paycheck to paycheck**. If you're spending every dollar you take home, you are, by definition, broke. More than 75% of Americans are living paycheck to paycheck, with little to no savings, which means that, right off the bat, at least three-quarters of us are impoverished. Even if you're not living paycheck to paycheck, though, you might still be broke if:

2. **You have credit-card debt**. There's no such thing as "good" debt: the debtor is always slave to the lender.

3. **You have student-loan debt**. Read our lips: THERE'S NO SUCH THING AS "GOOD" DEBT, DAMMIT!

4. **You have a monthly car payment**. Ahem.

5. **Your income dictates your lifestyle**. It should be the other way around: we should work to earn enough money to live, not live to earn enough money to buy shit we don't need. Until one breaks free from consumerism, the hoarder is slave to the hoard.

6. **You aren't saving for the future**. We know, we know: you'll start saving "tomorrow." But of course tomorrow never comes, because tomorrow will be today tomorrow, and tomorrow's tomorrow will never be today. Thus, begin today—your life literally depends on it.

7. **You're not healthy**. Unhealthy equals depression. Yes, if you're unhealthy, statistics show you're likely depressed. If you can't enjoy life, no matter how wealthy you are, then you're broke in a different way: you're *broken*. The richest man in the graveyard might have the most lavish tombstone, but he's still dead.

8. **Your relationships are suffering**. Too often we forsake the most important people in our lives in search of money or ephemeral pleasures. We believe our loved ones will always be around or that "they'll understand." But when you're careless with something for long enough, it breaks.

9. **You argue over money**. Troubled relationships tend to end for one of two reasons: arguments over money or arguments over sex (or both). Even if the relationship doesn't end, it is difficult to grow if you're constantly

bickering about finances. (P.S. If you're arguing over sex—
or the lack thereof—then something's *broke*n.)

10. **You're not growing**. It doesn't matter how much cash
you earn; if you're not growing, you're dying. We feel most
alive when we cultivate a passion, drudge through the
drudgery, and live our lives with purpose, autonomy, and
mastery.

11. **You don't contribute as much as you'd like**. Your
worth isn't determined by your net worth. Real worth
comes from contributing beyond yourself in a meaningful
way. It was Martin Luther King, Jr., who said, "Life's most
persistent and urgent question is: what are you doing for
others?"

Being broke is okay. Being broke without a plan to break
the cycle is *not*. We've all been broke at some point.

We all need money to live, but you are not the contents of
your wallet. What's more important than income is how we
spend the resources we have. We personally know broke
people who make six (or even seven) figures a year. We
also know families who live on $25,000 per year but aren't
broke at all because they live within their means—they live
deliberately.

Real wealth, security, and contentment come not from the
trinkets we amass, but from how we spend the one life
we've been given.

IMPORTANT THINGS WE PUT OFF
by Joshua Fields Millburn

No one likes to talk about death, and yet we're all going to die—obviously. Which makes for a strange paradox.

What's worse is we often refuse to discuss important topics surrounding death, like burial plans, cremation, living wills, and the like. The younger we are, the more we pretend the inevitable isn't inevitable.

And so we go about our day-to-day lives with these small little worries in the back of our minds, unsure what would happen if we got sick, if we died unexpectedly, if we became unconscious and could no longer make decisions for ourselves.

But that could never happen to me! we think, knowing full well it could, and it might. Young or old, we're all one brief moment away from a disaster.

We don't need to be afraid, though—we just need to be prepared.

I was *un*prepared for many, many years. Recently, though, I took worry by the hand and faced the fact that, at any time, I'm a moment away from death. So I decided to plan accordingly by obtaining or updating the following:

Living will. A living will, also known as an Advance Health Care Directive or Advance Medical Directive, is a legal document that provides your family, doctors, and caregivers with information about what life-saving measures you wish to be taken should there come a time when you are unable to communicate your wishes.

Last will and testament. A last will and testament is a legal document that dictates what happens to your estate once you pass away. If you have a complicated estate, it's best to have an attorney help you write your last will and testament, so you can be sure your estate is handled properly. If your situation is relatively straightforward, you can draft your own last will and testament and avoid attorney fees. It's best to learn about the components of a last will and testament and how to make sure yours is legally viable.

Power of attorney. As an independent adult, it's important for you to have a will. But something else you must consider is a power of attorney. This document legally allows a chosen person to be in charge of your financial matters (such as conducting bank transactions and investing money), property matters (such as management of property), and other legal situations (such as operating a small business). A power of attorney is not only used in cases of disability and illness, but also in cases where you can't be somewhere to sign a legal document.

Organ donor. See my essay about the importance of becoming an organ donor, "Here, Have an Organ," in the "Contribution" chapter of this book.

Although I intend to live for a long time, my deathbed ducks are now in a row. Even better, the worry has disappeared from the back of my mind. There are other documents and considerations you might want to consider, but the above four routes are a great start toward calm waters and a calm mind.

I used uslegalforms.com for some of the above documents,

as well as for other basic legal documentation needs. There are also free online resources like wikiHow.com that can point you in the right direction. For more complex taxation or legal matters, I seek the counsel of my CPA or attorney.

CAN'T FIX THE PROBLEM WITH THE PROBLEM

Suffice it to say, our economy is already broken. This isn't hard to see when we step out from among the pines and peer at the forest from a distance.

The problem is we're attempting to fix the problem *with* the problem. We're attempting to "stimulate" an economy that is already overstimulated, which is tantamount to giving a bottle of Jack Daniel's to a man with a hangover.

The economy is not what needs to be fixed, and capitalism is not broken. Neither "problem" is the real problem; rather, *we* are the problem. We have turned ravenous and self-indulgent, and, as a result, we are less happy than ever. Suicide rates are at an all-time high. Personal debt is at an all-time high. Stress, anxiety, discontent—all at all-time highs.

Collectively, over many years, we told ourselves (with conviction) we could buy happiness, so we manufactured a false economy based on rapacious over-spending and accumulating stuff we didn't need. And now it's the morning after the party and we're staring at ourselves in the mirror, unsure of how to make this pounding headache GO AWAY!

That bottle of Jack won't fix the problem—it will only make it worse. Stimulating the economy won't help, either. Changing how we live—*how we think about consuming, how we make decisions*—will slowly fix the problem. It will take time and action, but if enough of us live more deliberately, then we can fix this mess by fixing ourselves.

No, not everyone is going to become a minimalist: not everyone is going to live intentionally. But if we base our lives on the average person's life, then we're almost guaranteed to be unhappy—because the average person is unhappy.

We needn't, however, settle for someone else's discontent.

CHAPTER FIVE || **Mindfulness**

THE WORST THING THAT COULD HAPPEN

Risk scares the crap out of people. Many of us associate risk with failure, failure with pain. Yet we're told we must take plenty of risks to succeed. Thus, success must be painful, right?

Not necessarily.

When it comes to challenging our preconceived notions about risk, the common platitudinal question tossed around by kindhearted friends and self-help gurus is, "What's the worst thing that could happen?"

Truth be told, some risks are fairly benign: letting go of most of your material possessions, asking a cute guy or girl for his or her phone number, writing the first page of the book you've always wanted to write. What's the worst thing that could happen? Likely, nothing at all. There is no real risk in these harmless endeavors.

Other risks, however, probably *should* scare the shit out of you: skydiving, purchasing a home, quitting your job. What's the worst thing that could happen? Some pretty awful shit, actually: death, debt, and poverty, respectively. That doesn't mean you shouldn't take these risks, it means you should approach each risk with logic, reason, and intuition. Peer over the edge before taking your proverbial leap, and if it makes sense, then leap—because *not* leaping can be a much bigger risk.

The difference, then, between the benign risks and the real risks, is that the latter possesses potentially life-altering worst-case consequences, while the former poses virtually no threat at all.

When you think about it, though, the benign risks can also hold life-altering consequences if you change the question: What is the best—not the worst, but the *best*—thing that could happen? Perhaps getting rid of your excess stuff will free up time, money, space, and give you much-needed peace of mind. Perhaps that phone number will lead to a fulfilling relationship. Perhaps writing that first page will lead to a second, and then a third, and so on until you're staring at a bestseller. Any of these outcomes would likely change your life for the better.

Similarly, the real risks can have tremendous upsides. Jumping from a plane could be the most exhilarating experience of your life, the first time you've truly felt alive. A new home might be ideal for your family, a place in which you enjoy meaningful experiences, an investment. Walking away from your career could be the catalyst toward starting your own business, or a life of growth and contribution (it was both for us).

That doesn't mean you *should* undertake any of these risks, either—it just means we must ask these two questions more frequently. After all, what's the worst or best thing that could happen if we did?

DECLUTTERING YOUR MENTAL CLUTTER
by Ryan Nicodemus

Those voices inside your head won't be quiet: all you can hear is your boss telling you to have those reports complete by Friday, or your daughter reminding you there's soccer practice this Saturday, or a parent's voice telling you they need your help cleaning the house this weekend.

Most of us have somewhere to be each day, not to mention the everyday fire drills we get put through at work or at home. It can feel very overwhelming, and our minds can get noisy. Some of us even have echoes of voices from experiences from the past.

How do you deal with all that mental clutter?

Mental clutter is something I've worked on my entire life. I used to feel like, no matter what, I constantly had some sort of mental clutter—I always had something going on in my mind. If it wasn't something new causing that anxious, chaotic feeling, it was something from the past creeping back into the present to haunt me. Some days were worse than others, but it was there every day.

And then, after fixing several other parts of my life, I was able to cut down on the mental clutter:

Health. Your mind and your body aren't standing in separate corners of the room: it's much easier for a physically unhealthy person to experience a poor mental state. The brain is a delicate organ and we must treat it right. If you are interested in learning more, I recommend *Change Your Brain, Change Your Life* by Daniel G. Amen. I was impressed with Amen's in-depth explanation of the ties between the human brain and the human body.

I notice I feel more anxious when I have an empty stomach, have not exercised in a few days, eat junk food, and don't get enough sleep. I discovered once I changed these things, the mental clutter began clearing away.

Improving my health was an important first step.

Circumstances. If you're like me—the old me—then you're saying to yourself you can't change your circumstances. And with that attitude, we're right.

Once I decided I'd had enough of the mental clutter, though, I had no choice but to change my circumstances—I had no choice but to remove myself from circumstances that added to the problem.

I stopped associating with certain people, changed my spending habits, downsized my possessions. I started with myself, and, in time, changed my circumstances.

Over time things change, and instead of letting them change on their own, or letting things change me, I decided to change myself.

Some of those changes were difficult.

I stopped associating with a few folks who encouraged bad habits, and the world didn't stop spinning.

I was laid off from my six-figure career, and I didn't die.

I set new expectations with friends and family, and they supported me.

My circumstances are completely different now from what they were a short while ago, and I'm infinitely happier. Don't take this the wrong way: I'm not suggesting everyone needs to quit their job or take dire actions, but please understand your problems likely aren't as bad as you think.

Don't be fooled by anyone: you are in control of your circumstances; you are in control of you.

Past troubles. This was one of my biggest issues: my haunting past. I've made mistakes, I've let people down, and I've made dumb decisions. I've been extremely hard on myself, unnecessarily hard, neurotic about the mistakes and bad decisions I've made.

I'd often fall asleep replaying my whole day in my head, searching every interaction and conversation for mistakes so I could improve myself.

Now every time I feel anxiety caused from some past experience, I ask myself a few different questions: Is that situation relevant now? Was that situation even that serious? Am I blowing it out of proportion? Was that situation in my control? Does what that person, family member, or friend said actually have validity, or are they just acting out?

These questions helped me discern the things that mattered and didn't matter, so I could stop being so hard on myself. I also had to learn what things were in and out of my control. If something was out of my control, I accepted it so I could focus on the things I could control—the things I could change.

What makes you tick? To find out what made me tick, I drew a vertical line down a piece of paper. I labeled the left side "Bad Days" and the right side "Good Days." For each scenario, "Good Day" or "Bad Day," I thought of the foods I ate, people I saw, places I visited, etc. I couldn't remember every detail, but it gave me a few places to start.

To get better, I knew I needed to identify the problems, and then find the appropriate tools to combat them. Those tools can be different for everyone, but don't expect to fight the voice in your head on your own.

FIGHTING THE VOICE IN YOUR HEAD
by Joshua Fields Millburn

Although I read a lot of books, I tend to avoid recommending specific books for fear of boring others with my obsessions and personal preferences. However, I've gone out of my way to recommend Dan Harris's book, *10% Happier: How I Tamed the Voice in My Head, Reduced Stress Without Losing My Edge, and Found Self-Help That Actually Works—A True Story*, on social media and at our own book-tour stops. I've even gifted copies to friends who have been interested in mindfulness but haven't been able to get past the woo-woo often associated with meditating.

For the uninformed, Dan Harris is a co-anchor of *Nightline* and the weekend edition of *Good Morning America* on ABC. Covering wars in Afghanistan, Israel, Palestine, and Iraq, he has reported from all over the world and has produced investigative reports in Haiti, Cambodia, and the Congo. Dan also spent many years covering religion in America for *ABC World News with Peter Jennings*, despite not practicing a particular faith.

Like me, Dan used to scoff at meditation, assuming it was "for people who lived in yurts or collected crystals or had too many Cat Stevens records." But then, after suffering an on-air panic attack, he discovered considerable benefits from meditating. Described as a "deeply skeptical odyssey through the strange worlds of spirituality and self-help … a way to get happier that is truly achievable," *10% Happier*, which reached #1 on the *New York Times* bestseller list, chronicles one man's chaotic journey toward mindful living.

Dan was kind enough to discuss *10% Happier* and the practice of meditation with me for our readers.

JFM: What you've done with this book—at least for me—is make meditation accessible to the average person. The message is simple: anyone—be it a pant-suited businesswoman, a soccer dad, or Joe Sixpack—can benefit from meditation. Was that the reason you wrote *10% Happier*?

Dan: 100%! (Sorry. Lame math joke.) Meditation has a huge PR issue. I'd always been under the impression that it was only for freaks, weirdos, robed gurus, and people who are deeply into aromatherapy and Ultimate Frisbee. What changed my mind was learning that there's an enormous amount of science suggesting meditation is really good for you, and can do everything from lowering your blood pressure to boosting your immune system to literally rewiring key parts of your brain. I was also reassured to learn that meditating doesn't require lighting incense, chanting, sitting in a funny position, joining a cult, believing in anything, or wearing special outfits. The problem is, the way meditation has been traditionally presented in this country is too often syrupy and annoying—and leaves too many of us out of the conversation. I'm hoping to play a small role in changing that.

JFM: Yes, you are—particularly by providing people a story with which they can relate. Although your publisher doesn't promote *10% Happier* as a memoir, its well-crafted prose and narrative structure is certainly mimetic of that genre. Was the storytelling aspect of this book—compared to the self-help genre's standard prescriptive format—an important aspect for effectively communicating your message?

Dan: In my day job in television, I've learned time and again that the most powerful way to make a point is to illustrate it through the people's personal stories. (I've also read about studies showing that public health messages tend to be more effective when woven into narratives as opposed to delivered in a straight, informational way.) So I decided to take that approach with the book. Mind you, it wasn't easy. In order to illustrate how meditation changed my internal life, I really had to pull back the curtain and reveal some embarrassing stuff. I struggled mightily with that. In the end, though, I'm glad I did it, because it seems like the book has been useful to some people.

JFM: The book's central thesis is captured in its subtitle: *How I Tamed the Voice in My Head, Reduced Stress Without Losing My Edge, and Found Self-Help That Actually Works—A True Story*. Besides taming the inner voice and reducing stress, how else has meditation benefited your life?

Dan: The big thing that the subtitle leaves out is that meditation can make you a nicer person. It shows up on the brain scans: meditation literally grows the gray matter in the area of the brain associated with compassion. I can feel this happening with me a little bit. Mind you, I am far from perfect. If you were interviewing my wife, she'd be giving you her "he's 90% still a moron" spiel.

JFM: Ha! Let's talk about the title you originally proposed for the book: *The Voice in My Head Is an Asshole*. This resonated with me because it seems like we're all walking around with overwhelming amounts of mental clutter—that ADD-riddled inner voice who just won't shut up. Do you think it's always been this way—as humans we've always struggled with mental clutter? Has the suffusive nature of technology made our inner voices louder and more Tourettic?

Dan: I suspect that if you went back in time and interviewed people at various points in history, they'd all tell you that their era was the most stressful ever. And while there are plenty of reasons why today's world is uniquely anxiogenic, I am loath to argue that it's worse than, say, during World War II or, for that matter, the Civil War. Having issued that caveat, though, I do think that living in the age of "info-overload" can make us extremely frazzled. In particular, I have become a huge critic of multitasking—

which is really a short way of saying "doing many things poorly." Neurologically, it is impossible for us to focus on more than one thing at a time. But trying to focus these days, in the age of tweets, texts, and status updates, can be extremely tricky. Meditation—in which you repeatedly try to bring your attention to your breath in the face of your fizzing, looping mind—can really help with this.

JFM: Let's discuss meditation. Specifically, meditation as an act. I like to say I don't write *how-to* books, I write *why-to* books. And you seem to have done the same thing with *10% Happier*. Because you shine a spotlight on the benefits, it is easy to understand why we should meditate. Meditation itself, however, isn't easy: it is simple, but not easy. In the book, it becomes excruciatingly apparent during your 10-day silent retreat.

So, why do you think meditation is so difficult, especially for beginners? And, once someone knows they want to meditate—once they understand the benefits—what's a good way to get started?

Dan: Meditation is difficult for most of us because we're fighting a lifetime of habit. We've let the voice in our head —our thoughts, urges, and impulses—run amok. In meditation, you're attempting to rein that voice in, through the simple yet radical act of just focusing on your breath. But the fact that it's hard doesn't need to be a big problem. The whole game is to get lost in thought and start again … and again … and again. And every time you do that, it's a bicep curl for your brain. Seriously. The results even show up on MRI scans.

JFM: Thanks for your time, Dan. Any final words?

Dan: Meditation presents a radical notion: that our happiness doesn't have to depend on external factors. Happiness, it turns out, is a skill—one that you can train, just like you train your body in the gym. This is the next big public health revolution. Get on board.

HOW TO START MEDITATING

1. **Instruction**. Download free instructions from someone like Sam Harris (TheMinimalists.com/sam). You can also pay a few bucks and get the excellent Headspace app.

2. **Five minutes**. Start with just five minutes a day. Even if you have 23 children and fourteen jobs, you definitely have five minutes. Right after you wake up, right before you go to bed, or when you pull your car into the driveway before heading into your home for the night. Set an alarm on your phone and let rip.

3. **Give yourself a break**. Don't fall for the misconception you must "clear the mind." The only way you'll stop thinking is if you're dead—or enlightened. And don't worry if you're finding yourself getting lost: the whole game is finding the grit to start over.

SAM HARRIS DISCUSSES MINDFULNESS
by Joshua Fields Millburn

Sam Harris is the author of several bestselling books and winner of the 2005 PEN Award for Nonfiction. He is a cofounder and the CEO of Project Reason, a nonprofit foundation devoted to spreading scientific knowledge and secular values in society. He received a degree in philosophy from Stanford University and a Ph.D. in neuroscience from UCLA. Don't let the credentials scare you, though—he's an awesome guy.

Waking Up: A Guide to Spirituality Without Religion, Sam's newest book, is part seeker's memoir, part exploration of the scientific underpinnings of spirituality. No other book marries contemplative wisdom and modern science in this way, and no author other than Sam Harris—a scientist, philosopher, and famous skeptic—could write it.

Sam was kind enough to discuss *Waking Up* and mindfulness with me for *The Minimalists*.

JFM: At its onset, *Waking Up* introduces a common dilemma: "How can someone's happiness increase when all material sources of pleasure and distraction have been removed?" The thesis of my books is similar: we are focused on the wrong things, or perhaps we're not *focused* at all. Your solution: change the quality of your mind. Is this what you mean by "waking up"?

Sam: That's part of it. It's certainly true that our minds largely determine the quality of our lives. I'm not saying that outward circumstances don't matter—you and I can both be very grateful that we aren't living in Syria at this moment—but once a person has his basic needs met, how he uses his attention in every moment will spell the difference between happiness and misery. In particular, the habit of spending nearly every waking moment lost in thought leaves us at the mercy of whatever our thoughts happen to be. Meditation is a way of breaking this spell. Focus is one aspect of this: One discovers that concentrating—on *anything*—is intrinsically pleasurable. But there is more to meditation than just being focused.

JFM: Until recently, I found much value in single-task meditative experiences (walking, yoga, rock-climbing), but never turned to actual meditation until two books changed my view: *Waking Up* and another book you recommended, Dan Harris's (no relation) *10% Happier*. I interviewed Dan recently about why he turned to meditation to calm the voice in his head, and his experience resonated because he was able to remove the Eckhart Tolle–esque woo-woo that had always kept me from considering meditation as an answer to mental clutter. Your book, however, reverberated for a different reason: while Dan's book was a practical guide, *Waking Up* takes a deeper dive, an investigative, scientific approach to meditation, in which all assertions can be tested in the "laboratory of the mind." Can you expand on the differences between *meditation* and *meditative experience*? And, from a neuroscientist's point of view, why is meditation important for everyone?

Sam: I loved Dan's book, and I also interviewed him on my blog, SamHarris.org. Of course, there are different levels at which one can engage a practice like "mindfulness" (which Dan and I both discuss in our books). For many people, it will be like an executive stress ball—a tool for feeling a little better and improving one's performance. However, if one becomes deeply involved in the practice, it becomes more like the Large Hadron Collider—a means of discovering something fundamental, in this case about the nature of our minds. Perhaps the most important thing one can discover through the practice of meditation is that the "self"—the conventional sense of being a subject, a thinker, an experiencer living inside one's head—is an illusion.

And this is where meditative insight actually makes contact with science: because we know that the self is not what it seems to be. There is no place in the brain for a soul or an ego to be hiding. And it is possible to examine this illusory self closely enough to have the feeling that we call "I" disappear. As it happens, this comes as quite a relief.

JFM: Your writing—your books and your blog—beautifully combines humor, pathos, and intellectual prowess and has the rare ability to shift my perspective on a variety of topics such as drugs, gun control, violence, and morality. Compared to the rest of your body of work, how is *Waking Up* different?

Sam: It is definitely a more personal book. In terms of its scientific and philosophical message, it is also unconventional. I've come to these questions by a strange route. I dropped out of college and spent my twenties deeply immersed in the study of meditation and its associated literature. I then returned to school and got a degree in philosophy and a Ph.D. in neuroscience. After September 11, 2001, I spent a decade doing my best to call attention to the conflict between science and faith-based religion. This background allows me to approach the topic of spirituality from an unusual angle.

Most scientists and philosophers reject introspection as an intellectual tool, and most long-term meditators have little understanding of science. When you do find the rare scientist who has a serious meditation practice, he or she is unlikely to be especially aware of the problem of religion—hence many become boosters for Western Buddhism, or for the supposed underlying unity of all faiths. In *Waking Up*, I do my best to cut a new path through this wilderness. The self really is an illusion—and realizing this is the basis of spiritual life. But there is nothing that need be accepted on faith to accomplish this. We can have our cake (reason, skepticism, intellectual honesty) and eat it, too.

JFM: Approaching spirituality without religion can be confusing to believers and non-believers alike. In our culture, spirituality seems to be synonymous with faith, so much so it's hard to untangle the term and use it in any other context. And yet you do so masterfully, taking a rational approach to spiritual life, though it requires a considerable amount of unpacking to navigate the landscape around pseudo-spirituality and pseudo-science. So: why not use a nomenclature with fewer limitations? In the book's endnotes, you mention Christopher Hitchen's use of the term *numinous*, which sounds equally as appropriate—and beautiful—but without the contextual baggage.

Sam: This was one of those rare instances in which the right words simply don't exist in English. Many of my fellow scientists object to the term "spirituality"—because it has been so often associated with a belief in immaterial souls or spirits, magic, and so forth. They insist that I should confine myself to terms like "awe," "love," and "happiness." The problem, however, is that these words don't cover the same terrain. Almost everyone knows what it is like to feel awe at the beauty of the night sky, to love their kids, or to feel genuinely happy (if only for a short time). But these states of mind are not the same as self-transcendence. Nor do they indicate how subtle and transformative the investigation of one's own mind can be. Unfortunately, "numinous" doesn't do the job either (nor was Hitch talking about the kinds of insights and experiences I describe in my book). I'm certainly not happy with "spiritual"—and I do my best to strip it of its embarrassing associations early in the book. I also use the term "contemplative," which more clearly indicates that all of this has to be put into practice. But if one wants to quickly name the project of becoming like the Buddha, or Jesus, or some other celebrated yogi or sage—that is, recapitulating their first-person insights in a 21st century context without believing any bullshit —"spirituality" seems unavoidable, provided you make it clear that you're not talking about the power of crystals.

JFM: Much of *Waking Up* is laced with your personal life lessons, from experimenting with psychedelic drugs to spending years traveling Asia learning meditation with Buddhist and Hindu teachers. You discuss how we spend our lives in a "neurotic trance," one in which we "shop, gossip, argue, and ruminate our way to the grave," as well as how often we fail to appreciate what we have until we've lost it: "We crave experiences, objects, relationships, only to grow bored with them. And yet the cravings persist." Why is this our default setting, and how does it keep us from being truly happy?

Sam: There are many levels on which to answer that question. In evolutionary terms, we're probably lucky that we're not more miserable than we are. After all, our genes haven't been sculpted with our subjective well-being in mind. And the natural world surely wasn't created for our enjoyment. We've evolved to survive and spawn—to just barely equip our progeny to do the same. All the other good things in life appear to be lucky accidents.

In large part, our problems are due to the immense power of language. We live in a world that is almost entirely defined by words—our relationships, fears, interests, cultural institutions, the very objects around us are all the product of concepts that depend upon language. And this is no less true of our inner lives. Thinking is so useful that we are probably wired to do it continuously. Unfortunately, much of what we think about makes us miserable.

To take a very simple example: Most people are very concerned about their social status, a preoccupation we share with our primate cousins. Unlike baboons, however, we can truly brood about our failures, projecting them into a recollected past and an imagined future. What's more, we can do this in an ever-widening context of social knowledge. If you're a baboon, at least you can seize the alpha male by the throat and try your luck. But when you're on the Internet, contemplating the splendor of others—"Oh, Gwyneth Paltrow is spending Christmas on St. Barts, how nice…."—the odds are against your feeling fully satisfied with your place in the world. Millions of years of hominid evolution have not prepared us for Instagram.

JFM: Once I understood the importance of mindfulness in my own life, your guided meditations (TheMinimalists.com/sam) helped me better understand how to meditate effectively. Your wife, Annaka, has successfully taught mindfulness practice to children as young as six. Is it harder for a 33-year-old guy like myself to "wake up," compared to, say, an elementary-school child? Should parents encourage their children to meditate?

Sam: Mindfulness is an extremely useful tool for kids—just teaching them to be aware of their emotions is an important step toward basic sanity. But it probably requires an adult mind to discover the true power of the practice. So I think we've got an edge over the kids.

JFM: The benefits of awareness are extraordinary. I believe your book, and mindfulness in general, will help people, as you say, "escape the usual tides of psychological suffering"—the crippling fear and anger and shame that ruin our present moment—by illuminating everyone's ability to be free in the midst of whatever is happening. While this appears to be the primary benefit of spirituality, what other benefits have you experienced from mindfulness?

Sam: There have been at least four or five occasions on which I've managed not to send a tweet...

JFM: I'll see you at your Waking Up with Sam Harris Lecture Series in September. After embarking on a 100-city book tour this year myself, I now understand the benefits of face-to-face interaction with readers. What do you hope to accomplish with these live events that can't be achieved by just reading your book?

Sam: A proper conversation. This is one of the true frustrations of being a writer: Your words get absorbed in your absence—often to unintended effect. At these events, I'll make my case for a rational spirituality for an hour and then spend another hour cleaning up the mess in a Q&A. Then we'll all start drinking. So wish me luck.

JFM: Good luck. And thank you for your time. Any final words?

Sam: Your mind is all you truly have. So it makes sense to train it.

5 WAYS TO CREATE SOLITUDE
by Joshua Fields Millburn

Our daily lives are filled with noise. Every day it's getting harder to turn down the volume.

Even the places in which we used to find brief stints of solitude have been enveloped by our heavily mediated culture: airport waiting-rooms pipe "info-tainment" into our heads via overhead HD monitors, grocery-store check-out lines drip soul-crushing pop music into our ears, and even bookstores (what's left of them) bombard us with ambient advertisements and visual clutter at every turn.

And don't even get me started on the things within our control, things like the TVs in our homes, our Internet connections, our smartphones, our iPads, and our infinite technical "advances," most of which cocoon our attention spans every waking moment of every day.

Often the noise feels inescapable, un-turn-down-able, utterly overwhelming—the only way to avoid it seems to be while we're sleeping. Or does it invade our dreams, too?

But there's good news: we can turn down the noise. It's not always easy, and it takes a certain kind of awareness, but we can turn it down. It is our choice.

I've found at least five ways to create solitude in chaotic times.

1. **Wake early**. Wake slowly. Take your time. Think. I write in the mornings in a quiet room with no distractions—no TV, no radio, no clocks, no noise: just me and my thoughts and the words on the page.

2. **Schedule time to read**. I love reading, especially literary fiction. It was a way for me to force myself into solitude: just me and my thoughts and the characters on the page.

3. **Go for a walk**. I walk all the time. Walking gives me uninterrupted time to think, time for myself, time inside my head to marshal my thoughts and emotions. Even if it's a fifteen minute walk, it's worth my time: just me and my thoughts and the city lights under Midwest skies.

4. **Exercise**. I exercise every day. Sometimes I go to the gym. Sometimes I do push-ups, squats, and pull-ups in the park. Whatever I do, I have the opportunity to do it by myself in solitude: just me and my thoughts and my body in motion.

5. **Get rid of distractions**. This sounds like common sense, but we're so distracted by the noise that common sense doesn't seem all that common these days. But you can try to turn off your cellphone for a while, dump your television, kill the Internet for a month, get rid of a few clocks, check email and social networks only once a day, and find ways to

remove subtle distractions from your life. That's what I've done and it's great: just me, my thoughts, and a more meaningful life.

A QUIET PLACE
by Joshua Fields Millburn

My mind often cries for serenity.

When I moved to a mountainside cabin in Montana for four months, my intention was to tap into a pseudo–Walden Pond experience, one in which I was closer to nature, closer to myself—my *interior* self—than ever before.

It worked. During those months, I committed myself to a great deal of self-exploration, a great deal of writing (I wrote a ton of short stories, including "Echo Lake"), and a plethora of activities that forced me to better examine my interior life: tending to a fire for warmth, dealing with the loneliness of remote living, living more intentionally out of necessity.

One of my recent experiences—living with two single guys in Missoula, Montana's University District—more closely mimics Thoreau's experience than the remote cabin.

Hard to believe, right? The reason is simpler than one might guess: amid the talking, the visitors, the socializing, the work, the meetings, the stuff-30-year-old-single-guys-do, I found a serene place, a place all my own, a place to which I could retreat when I needed absolute peace.

That place was my bedroom.

Back in the cabin, peace and quiet became the norm. I was surrounded by deafening silence. But at the Asym House, I was forced to seek quiet when I was in need. Thus, I established my bedroom as my quiet place. Much like Thoreau's lakeside plot, my room contained only a few necessary items: a bed for sleeping, a desk for writing, a chair for sitting, and a lamp for reading. Occasionally, I burned a candle so my olfactory sense—our strongest sense—knew I was in my quiet place.

That's it—there was nothing else. I left the walls blank, the wood floor bare. I didn't want anything else in my quiet place. It needed to be not only quiet auditorily, but visually as well.

I'm not opposed to artwork adorning my walls nor decorations festooning my shelves. Aesthetics are important. Art and decorations often add a personal touch to a living space. But I can hang artwork and other personal embellishments anywhere in the home. My room, however, is intentionally void of these things. No clock, no paintings, no photos, no bookshelf, no nightstand, no noise. It's completely quiet, distraction-free, and thus it's anxiety- and stress-free, too.

How about you? Where is your quiet place?

ALONE TIME
by Joshua Fields Millburn

I'm walking through the Deep South, alone but not lonely.

I used to think there was something wrong with me. Throughout my twenties, I followed societal norms, doing all the things you're *supposed* to do to be a normal, functioning member of society: going out with co-workers after work, spending every evening and weekend with friends, killing time with insipid small talk. Always engaged. Always on. Never alone.

This constant interaction wore me out—I often wasn't pleasant to be around. It felt oddly lonely to never be alone.

Then, as my twenties twilighted, I discovered I was more affable whenever I carved out time for myself. (After all, I'm an INTJ on the Myers-Briggs Type Indicator personality test.) Don't worry, this isn't a trite reminder to "make time for yourself"; rather, it's a reminder to embrace your individualism—*your* personality.

Today I spend copious amounts of time by myself. I don't know anyone who spends more time alone than me. At least 80 percent of my time is spent solo—walking, writing, exercising, reading, ruminating. I've learned to enjoy silence; I've learned to sit quietly and hear what's going on not just around me, but inside myself.

Yet the greatest benefit of prolonged solitude is when I do decide to immerse myself in social situations—be it dinner with friends, a date, or on tour—I'm pretty awesome to be around. Not only do I benefit from my alone time, but everyone around me benefits, too. We all get the best version of me. I'm able to burst into social situations with stored energy, which actually makes most people believe I'm an extrovert since I'm able to engage at a high level, employing active listening, humor, and intellectually stimulating conversation.

I don't, however, recommend more alone time, or more social time, to anyone. Life is not one-size-fits-all, so what works for me may not work for you.

Take Ryan for example. As an ENFP, his personality is nearly the opposite of mine: he spends more time around people than anyone I know. He's the life of the party, naturally charismatic, funny, and likable. Always naturally on. As an extrovert he actually gets his energy from other people, and time alone exhausts him.

But classifying his approach, or my approach, as *right* or *wrong* misses the point. Both *can* be right—or wrong—depending on your personality, which is, of course, a continuum. Even I, and my introverted ways, would hate to be sentenced to perpetual solitary confinement, just as Ryan, and his charming extroversion, occasionally needs a break from his socialite lifestyle.

Ultimately, whether introvert or extrovert, man or woman, young or old, I recommend learning more about yourself. Because once you better know yourself, you can grow by easing into your discomfort zone.

(If you'd like to take it, you can find a free, attenuated

version of the Myers-Briggs Type Indicator test at
TheMinimalists.com/mbti.)

CHANNEL SURFING

We're always looking for something better. Something
nicer. Something faster. Something newer. Something
shinier. Something bigger. Something more. Something
else.

The remote control made this kind of searching easier than
ever. You can navigate a thousand channels without leaving
your couch, flipping endlessly through channel after
channel after channel until you find something *better*.

But television isn't the only place in which we constantly
search for something better. We flip through every aspect
of our lives—food, relationships, entertainment, work—all
the while looking for anything other than what's in front of
us.

The problem is, in a world of unlimited choices, there
actually *is* always something better somewhere on another
channel. So, even when we find something we like—
something we enjoy—it's never enough, and we begin to
yearn for something else.

The key is to be happy with the channel you're watching. If
you're not happy, take action, change the channel—work
hard to change your situation—but once you find
something you like, enjoy it. You needn't surf in perpetuity.

Once you enjoy your life you will grow, and eventually the channel will change on its own.

FOREVER DOES NOT EXIST

Everything is ephemeral: on a long enough timeline, everything ends.

The relationship you are in now will end. The happiness you will experience tomorrow will end. The depression you feel today will end. Even your life will eventually end. Nothing lasts forever, not even those diamonds in the advertisement.

Yet we live our lives like the best things will continue into perpetuity, like the good stuff will stick around and the bad stuff will go away once we obtain everything we want. But, good or bad, life is limited, everything is eventual, the ending is inevitable.

Feel warm and fuzzy yet? You should. The most important reason to live in the moment is nothing lasts forever. Enjoy the moment while it's in front of you. Be present. Accept life for what it is: a finite span of time with infinite possibilities.

Treat friends with utter respect. Treat your lover to your full attention. Treat today like it matters. Live in the moment.

Don't wait until a special occasion to show the people in your life you love them—if we wait until their birthdays, Christmas, or next week, the moment may never come—say the words and show it in your actions every day.

THE TROUBLING NATURE OF POP CULTURE

We've all been MTV'd. We grew up with pop drivel invading every dark corner of our media-saturated lives: The glowing box in the living room showcasing *ideal* families in *ideal* homes living *ideal* lives. The car stereo blaring bland top-40-isms during rush-hour traffic. Newspapers foretelling inescapable doom and irremediable despair without any hope of salvation or redemption. Magazines twaddling the latest gossip about *such and such* and *what's his name*.

Our collective brains have soaked up the meaningless muck and are now waterlogged with platitudes and cultural niceties and the false expectations of the way life should be.

American Express: Never leave home without it.
Coca-Cola: It's the real thing.
McDonald's: I'm lovin' it.

We know these corporate slogans—and many others—by heart. We've let them in without even knowing we were letting them in. We've accepted these mantras as maxims by which we should make our decisions.

If someone continuously repeats a lie, does it eventually become the truth? Is it not safe to leave our homes without our credit cards? Is the realest thing in our lives a carbonated aluminum can of sugar? Do we really *love* the golden arches?

Even Pringles admits they know we are programmed: *Once you pop, you can't stop!* Sadly, they're right. It's difficult to shake the sedative weight of everything we've learned from pop culture. Fortunately, though, once you go pop, you *can* stop.

We never opted-in to pop culture: it had us in its sinister clutch at birth, an invisible umbilical cord no one thought to cut.

After all, what's the harm in a little TV, in a little late-night news, in catching up on the day's current events? Nothing. But when we simply accept the idiot box's catchy one-liners as epigrams by which we must make our most important decisions, we get lost quickly.

It's easy to be passively entertained and informed, accepting catchphrases to be self-evident. Even the news has to be "info-tainment" these days so it's more palatable to the casual listener (read: consumer).

That's because it's easy to be entertained, but it's hard work to seek out the truth, it's difficult to form our own opinions based on multiple points of view, and it's much easier to allow someone else—be it Rush Limbaugh, Keith Olbermann, or a faceless corporation with a seemingly endless marketing budget—to form an opinion for us.

Besides the problems of its inherently passive nature, today's commercial-riddled pop-information can't inform us of life's larger problems, of our deepest troubles and fears, of what it actually means to be alive—what it means to be a human being in the most complex time in human history.

The American Dream is broken—it has been for decades, and attempting to go back to "the way things were" will not fix it. "Fixing it" would only perpetuate the inevitable, making it worse in the long run. The longer we put off our troubles, the harder they are to deal with.

Instead, as a culture, *we* must take responsibility. We must fix ourselves. We must create the disciplines necessary to be alive in this complex world. We must become *aware* of what's going on around us so ultimately we can be aware of what's going on *inside* us—only then will we know what's truly important.

COSTS AND BENEFITS OF AWARENESS
by Ryan Nicodemus

I'm standing half-nude in front of a full-length mirror, pinching and poking at my midsection.

Throughout the past two weeks I've been on a dietary cleanse—mostly raw foods, no alcohol, no caffeine, no processed foods, no animal products. I've also been hitting the gym each morning for a rigorous workout. Two fine improvements to my daily routine. Without a doubt, I'm healthier now than I was a month ago: Less body fat. More muscle. Better sleep. Most important, I feel great (how we feel is the best barometer of health).

So why am I more frustrated with the image staring back at me in the mirror?

Whenever we make radical changes—diet, exercise, career, etc.—we shine a spotlight on our flaws. Our blemishes glare back at us in the light—this is the cost of awareness. Our standards change whenever we are infected with a new awareness: we scrutinize ourselves more. The more we scrutinize, the more the spotlight brightens, and the more our imperfections stand out.

Awareness isn't always pleasant, but becoming aware is important and necessary: the benefits, especially the long-term benefits, can be experienced only once we've seen our flaws for what they are—past weaknesses. Only then can we work toward strengthening ourselves. Only then can we move toward the best version of ourselves.

True awareness allows us to improve, to grow—to become better, but not perfect. Our lives will never be perfect: we've all been cut deeply. That's okay. Awareness helps us heal, and our scars make up the best parts of us.

OFFBEAT
by Ryan Nicodemus

Sometimes I get into a rut. I feel stuck. Stagnant.

When I first moved to Missoula, Montana, I felt this way. I didn't have many friends, just a few acquaintances. One acquaintance invited me over for game night where a group of us sat around playing board games and drinking wine.

The get-together's host, Rebecca, was a theater director. When I asked how her most recent production, *Thisillusionment*, was coming along, she said, "Everything's great, except I can't find someone to fill the main role of Ivan the Magician."

Feeling the courage provided by three glasses of wine, I extended my arms in front of me, palms down, and then flipped my palms upward with exaggeration, rolled up my sleeves one-by-one, and said, with arms spread wide, "I think I might be the magician you're looking for." Rebecca laughed and said she'd let me audition for the role.

So I did.

I've never acted in a play, so I couldn't believe it when they offered me the lead role.

I spent the next eight weeks rehearsing, five days a week, four hours each evening, getting ready for the production. Without realizing it, I slowly moved out of my rut. The growth I experienced in just two months was astonishing; I've never grown that much in such a condensed period of time: I gained an exponential amount of acting experience, learned how a play was developed start-to-finish, and, most important, I made great friends with whom I now have a strong connection. I became unstuck.

A lot of my mentoring clients ask me how to get out of a rut. I tell them to change their physical state. I don't suggest all my clients audition for a play, but I do suggest they do something offbeat.

Diving into something new can be terrifying, or at least uncomfortable, but those feelings of discomfort are indicative of growth.

If you're stagnant or stuck, change your state. Do something offbeat: audition for a play, take a photography class, take tango lessons, do cartwheels in the yard. Whatever you do, do not continue the same old routine.

OVERCOMING SELF-DOUBT
by Ryan Nicodemus

There used to be this side of me that questioned every action I took, every word I spoke, every thought I had. I believed everything that occurred in—and around—my life was because of *my* actions, especially when it came to how other people felt about me. I thought I was in total control of other people's emotions—my words and actions determined if they were happy, sad, angry, or discontent. I eventually realized I was not in control of how others felt— not 100% in control, anyway.

But how could I tell the difference between when I did and I didn't have control over how others felt toward me?

Let's examine two extreme examples. Imagine I meet someone and give him a hug. This expression of kindness and love typically translates to just that: kindness and love. Now imagine I meet someone else and say, "Man, those skinny jeans make your butt look big." I wouldn't ever say that, but this action translates, without a doubt, into something completely different. Let's assume in the latter example my intentions were somehow good: perhaps I was attempting, inarticulately, to tell the person those jeans were simply not flattering. Irrespective of my intentions with either action, each one will draw a different response.

The trouble I run into is when my actions are filled with

good intentions, but the person interprets my actions in a different way. When this happens, I often sit and ask self-loathing, degrading questions—*What did I do wrong? How did they misunderstand me? Why am I such a moron?*—and I blame myself for being misunderstood.

Here's where I really confuse myself: sometimes I lay in bed at night recounting my day, and I suddenly recognize I could have approached a situation differently. Other times, I lay in bed and realize I couldn't have possibly been any clearer, kinder, or more considerate, which leads to even more negative self-talk: *People just don't understand you. You're weird and people don't get you no matter how hard you try. If you acted differently, maybe that person would like you.*

We all care about how others view us—sometimes too much. It used to be one of the only things that mattered to me, but I have been able to break this habit. I have been able to feel confident no matter how people treat me. I have been able to stop giving a damn about what people who don't like me think.

This is how I did it:

First, I had to recognize the language I use—the way I talk to myself—is crucial. When I experience negative emotions, it's easy to beat the hell out of myself with my words and perpetuate negative thoughts. This never does any good: negative self-talk is demoralizing and destructive. So I found new questions to ask myself—I found new ways to talk to myself.

I came up with different questions. Instead of

disempowering questions, I now ask myself five clarifying questions:

Did I have good intentions?
Did I do my best to communicate the message?
Was I as genuine as possible?
Was I honest in the message I was communicating?
Did I consider the other person's feelings before I spoke?

These questions help me determine, in a non-destructive way, if I need to rethink my approach. If I can answer *yes* to those five questions, then I needn't feel remorse or confusion about why the other person did not understand my intentions. If I cannot answer *yes*, I explore new ways to communicate my message differently.

Second, I had to tame my cynical side. Instead of destructive language, I now say things like, *Ryan, not everyone is judging you. Sometimes people have a hard time accepting the truth, good or bad. Their misunderstandings do not make them or me wrong or bad —it was just a misunderstanding. Maybe the next time you see that person they will be in a different mood and see things in a new light. You can't make everyone see your point of view or where you're coming from.*

When I don't agree with someone or when someone doesn't agree with me, it doesn't make them wrong or bad: it makes them who they are. It doesn't make me crazy or a moron: it makes me who I am. As much as I'd like to find a connection with everyone, it isn't realistic. Ultimately, the only person's expectations I must meet are mine.

CHAPTER SIX || **Gift-Giving**

WHEN TO GIVE GIFTS

Ours is a gift-giving culture, one that places great emphasis on giving physical items to other people as a measurement of caring. Seems silly to write, but it's the truth: we often give gifts to show we care.

So, on your birthday, and a handful of holidays, people show they care about you. Don't they care about you those other 350+ days every year? Or do they feel different about you those days because they aren't gifting a physical item (one you probably don't want, anyway)?

Let's face it—the worst time to give a gift is on a birthday or holiday: there is an invisible expectation to give gifts at these times, and it's a hard expectation to live up to.

The best time to give a gift is *today*. Right now, for absolutely no reason at all. This helps us show the people in our lives they are just as important to us today as they are on any holiday.

GIFT EXPERIENCES, NOT STUFF

Here's an idea: what if you decide to gift only experiences this year? How much more memorable will your holidays be?

Experiences worth considering: concert tickets, a home-cooked meal, tickets to a play or musical, breakfast in bed, a back rub, a foot rub, a full-body massage, a holiday parade, walking or driving somewhere without a plan, spending an evening talking with no distractions, making-out under the mistletoe, visiting a festival of lights, cutting down a Christmas tree, watching a sunrise, skiing, snowboarding, sledding, dancing, taking your children to a petting zoo, making snow angels, making a batch of hot apple cider, taking a vacation together, watching a wintertime sunset.

What other experiences can you give to someone you care about?

Your experiences build and strengthen the bond between you and the people you care about.

Don't you think you'd find more value in these experiences than material gifts? Don't you think your loved ones will find more value, too? There's only one way to find out.

LETTING GO OF PHYSICAL GIFTS

The two of us tend not to accept physical gifts. Sometimes it's hard to get people to understand this cultural shift. The best way to approach the no-gift-getting concept is to be proactive: we set the expectation with our friends and family we don't need any more stuff, and if they want to give us gifts, they can get us experiences we will enjoy; they can celebrate our lives with us by spending time with us, not by piling on more stuff.

Of course, most of us don't want to piss people off: we don't want to offend. We worry what others will think.

Case in point—we received an interesting email from a reader, Dena, about Joshua's essay, "Letting Go of Sentimental Items":

I recently started my minimalist journey, and up until now everything I have let go of has been pretty easy. I just wanted to thank you for this post because you helped me see that we are not our stuff. I now realize I do not have to hold on to something in order to remember a loved one; their memories are inside me. However, I am having trouble getting rid of gifts. It's not me who has a problem getting rid of them, it's the people who gave them to me who might get a bit upset. I was wondering if you had any suggestions? I want to get rid of this stuff because I feel like it is holding me up from moving on with my new lifestyle but I do not want to offend anyone.

Joshua's response:

Most people won't notice or won't care. A few might get offended, and that's okay.

When I left my corporate job, some people got offended. When I stopped checking email every day, some people got offended. When I said "no" to certain past commitments, some people got offended. When I untethered from negative relationships, some people got offended.

We can't let these things bother us, though. I think my friend Julien Smith said it best: *"Yes, it's really happening right at this moment. Some people don't like you, and guess what? There's nothing you can do about it. No amount of coercion, toadying, or pandering to their interests will help. In fact, the opposite is often true; the more you stand for something, the more they respect you, whether it's grudgingly or not. What people truly respect is when you draw the line and say, 'I will go no further.' They may not like this behavior, but so what? These people don't like you anyway, why should you attempt to please them?"*

It's okay to toss the stuff if it's not adding value to your life: donate it, sell it, recycle it. Let go of it so you can focus on what's important in your life. Most people won't even notice, especially the people who care about you.

THE COMMODIFICATION OF LOVE

There's always another holiday lurking somewhere around the corner: Valentine's Day. Mother's Day. Sweetest Day. Birthdays. Christmas. We've programmed ourselves to give and receive gifts on these and many other holidays to show our love for one another.

We've been told gift-giving is one of our "love languages." This is ridiculous, and yet we treat it as gospel: I love you—see, here's this expensive shiny thing I bought you.

Gift-giving is not a love language any more than Pig Latin is a Romance language; rather, gift-giving is a destructive cultural imperative in our society, and we've bought it (literally) hook, line, and sinker. We've become consumers of love.

The grotesque idea we can somehow commodify love is nauseating. We often give gifts to show our love because we are troubled by real love. Buying diamonds is not evidence of everlasting devotion: commitment, trust, understanding—these are indications of devotion.

Gift-giving is, by definition, transactional—but love is not a transaction. Love is transcendent: it transcends language and material possessions, and can be shown only by our thoughts, actions, and intentions.

Jonathan Franzen said it best: "Love is about bottomless empathy, born out of the heart's revelation that another person is every bit as real as you are. To love a specific person, and to identify with his or her struggles and joys as if they were your own, you have to surrender some of your self."

This doesn't mean there's something necessarily wrong with buying a gift for someone, but don't fool yourself by associating that gift with love—love doesn't work that way.

AN IRRESPONSIBLE CHRISTMAS

It's easy to see when we've arrived at the "holiday-shopping season." Take a look around: The shopping malls are packed with herds of consumers. The storefronts are decorated in green and red. The jingly commercials are running nonstop.

The holiday season has much to recommend it, though: each year around this time we all feel that warm-'n'-fuzzy Christmastime nostalgia associated with the onset of winter. We break out the scarves, the gloves, the winter coats. We go ice skating, we go sledding, we eat hearty meals with our extended families. We take days off work, spend time with our loved ones, give thanks for the gift of life.

The problem is we've been conditioned to associate this joyous time of year—the mittens, the decorations, and the family activities—with purchasing material items. We've trained ourselves to believe buying stuff is part of Christmas.

We all know, however, the holidays needn't require gifts to be special; rather, this time of year is special because of its true meaning—not the wrapped boxes we place under the tree.

There's nothing inherently wrong with gifts, but it's irresponsible for us to believe purchasing presents is a holiday requirement. Let's instead celebrate the infinite gifts all around us. Even without presents, we have everything we need to be jolly, merry, and joyous on Christmas.

LET'S TALK ABOUT BLACK FRIDAY

Here we are, in the midst of what is supposedly the most joyous time of year: the holiday season. And yet, for most of us, it's also the most stressful time of year. At some point, Santa Claus turned corporate and the holiday season metamorphosed into the holiday-*shopping* season.

Shopping. This one word, although birthed from a place of great intentions, has fundamentally changed our outlook from blissful to grim, from jolly to anxious, from *celebrating* Christmas to *surviving* the holidays. It's upsetting, and with consumption's vicious inertia, it seems there's no way for us to exit the speeding train of consumerism.

Black Friday is the busiest shopping day of the year. (Boxing Day is the overseas equivalent.) Retailers prepare months in advance for this dark day—preparation that's meant to stimulate our insatiable desire to consume: Doorbuster sales. New products. Gigantic newspaper ads. TV, radio, billboards. Sale, sale, sale! Early bird specials! One day only! Get the best deal! Act now! While supplies last. See store for details.

But as shiny as its facade may be, the harmful aspects of Black Friday are not few. The pandemonium that takes place on this day is perhaps a broader metaphor for our consumer culture as a whole. On this day we consume gluttonously without regard for the harm we're inflicting on ourselves. On this day greed becomes ravenous. On this day we live without real meaning, buying gifts to fill a void that can't possibly be filled with material possessions.

Black Friday is the day we trample people for things we don't need, the day after being thankful for what we have.

If you want to give gifts, why not gift an experience—a nice meal, tickets to a concert, or a sunset on the beach? The best, most loving gift you can give someone is your time and undivided attention. Presence is the best present.

If that doesn't work, buy everyone on your Christmas list a giant trash can so they can throw away all the presents they received, but didn't ask for.

40 REASONS TO AVOID BLACK FRIDAY
by Joshua Fields Millburn

Once upon a time (throughout my twenties) in a faraway land (Ohio and Kentucky), I managed a slew of retail stores. For a dozen years I traversed retail's murky waters. Fresh out of high school, I began my career as a bushy-tailed sales rep at age eighteen. A few years later I was promoted to sales manager. Then store manager. Eventually I climbed the rungs to regional manager and, finally, director. At my pinnacle, I managed the operations for 150 brick-and-mortar stores from my downtown corner office.

I learned a lot about the retail business during my tenure. Most notably, I grasped the importance of the holiday-shopping season. On a good year, my stores would reap as much as forty percent of their annual revenue in the five weeks between Thanksgiving and New Year's. Forty percent! That's manufactured demand at its best (worst). Completely unnatural. Steroidic.

Because the stakes were so high, we started planning months in advance for Black Friday and its proceeding weeks. We met weekly, devising plans for doorbuster sales, special deals, once-a-year offers—anything to herd bovine-like customers through the door.

Those so-called deals weren't designed for *your* benefit: we weren't strategizing hoping to find ways to save you money, to assist the cost-conscious single mom, to help the nuclear family create a more memorable Christmas. No, no, no. We scoured our plans for every possible way to *help*—help you part with your money, that is. The sale got you in the door, but the deal was not a deal at all.

The Black Friday deals aren't that good. They're designed to look appealing in the newspaper's free-standing insert, but the flip side is the deals are designed to get you to act on impulse. Retailers lure you in with a limited-time offer, and then coerce you into purchasing shit you don't need by creating false scarcity.

Don't succumb to the pressure: if it's worth buying on Black Friday, it's worth buying in January, too. You don't need forty reasons to avoid shopping on Black Friday, you need only one: you will have a much more meaningful holiday without extracting the plastic from your wallet.

Spend some time with the people you love next Black Friday. Share a meal. Find a Christmas tree. Enjoy a carriage ride. Go iceskating. Donate your time to a food bank. Dance under the bright downtown lights. Play in the snow (or in the sand). Or just relax and enjoy the holiday ~~shopping~~ season. Simply be together—no purchase necessary.

Will you join me? Will you avoid shopping on Black Friday? Or will you follow the crowd?

ASK FOR BETTER CHRISTMAS PRESENTS

You know that time of year: it's getting down to the wire— just a few weeks left until the big day when everyone unwraps their presents, drinks their eggnog, and complains about what they did and didn't get for Christmas.

We at *The Minimalists* have already written extensively about the gifts we like to receive: experiences, love, and time. We'd be remiss, however, if we didn't discuss the gift of *giving*, the gift of *contribution*.

The old saying is true: 'tis better to give than to receive. We get so much more by giving.

A few months ago, Ryan gave his birthday to charity and raised enough money to build a well in Cambodia. Instead of accepting material birthday gifts, he was able to gift clean water to more than 250 people who didn't previously have access to it.

Perhaps you can do the same this Christmas: instead of requesting gifts, you can ask people to donate to your favorite charity in your name. Don't have a favorite charity? Consider asking people to donate to charitywater.org: they make it easy for you to set up your own page, and 100% of all donations go to bringing clean water to people who need it—people who might die without it.

Wouldn't that feel better than a new neck tie, a new pair of shoes, or a new piece of jewelry?

THE WORST CHRISTMAS EVER

It's Christmas Day. Little Andy tears off wrapping paper to reveal Optimus Prime. He smiles as the large robot toy comes to life with flashes and beeps. Andy's parents' expressions, however, are more pained grimaces than smiles as the toy twirls away.

A few minutes later, Andy discards the toy and begins unwrapping the rest of his presents, extracting each box from under the tree, one by one—some long, some tall, some heavy, some light. Each box reveals a new toy. Each shred of green-and-red wrapping paper, a flash of happiness.

An hour later, however, little Andy is crying hysterically. Based on his fits, this has undoubtedly been the Worst. Christmas. Ever. Sure, Andrew received many of the things on his list—but he's far more concerned with what he didn't receive. The toys in front of him simply remind him of what he doesn't have.

Sounds childish, but we do the same thing: we look at things around us and want more. We covet the neighbor's new car, the co-worker's new clothes, the friend's new iPhone.

What if Andy was happy with the toys in front of him? What if we were, too?

CHAPTER SEVEN || **Priorities**

REAL PRIORITIES

Take a look at your day-to-day life.

Through the hustle and bustle of your daily grind, what banal, tedious, mundane tasks eat up most of your time? Checking email? Monkeying around on Facebook? Watching television? Filling out reports?

Whatever your answer, these activities are your *true* priorities.

We often claim our priorities are grandly important activities like spending time with family, exercising, or carving out enough alone time to work on that big passion project we've been putting off. Unless you're actually putting these pursuits first, unless you make these undertakings part of your everyday routine, they are not your actual priorities.

Your priorities are what you do each day, the small tasks

that move forward the second and minute hands on the clock: these circadian endeavors are your *musts*. Everything else is simply a *should*.

NOT BUSY, FOCUSED
by Joshua Fields Millburn

Take a look around: everyone is multitasking. We're doing more than we've ever done, attempting to fill every interstitial zone with more work. Every downtown scene is the same: heads tilted downward, faces lost in glowing screens, technology turning people into zombies.

We live in a busy world, one in which our value is often measured in productivity, efficiency, work rate, output, yield, GTD, the rat race. We are inundated with meetings and spreadsheets and status updates and rush-hour traffic and tweets and conference calls and travel time and text messages and reports and voicemails and multitasking and all the trappings of a busy life. Go, go, go. Busy, busy, busy.

Americans are working more hours than ever, but we are actually earning less. *Busy* has become the new norm. If you're not busy, especially in today's workplace, you're often thought of as lazy, unproductive, inefficient, a waste of space.

For me, *busy* is a curse word. I grimace whenever someone accuses me of being busy, my facial features contorting and writhing in mock pain. I respond to this accusation the same way each time: "I'm not busy, I'm focused."

Henry David Thoreau said, "It is not enough to be busy. The question is: what are we busy about?" If I were to append his quandary, I'd say, "It is not enough to be busy. The question is: what are we focused on?"

There is a vast difference between being busy and being focused. The former involves the typical tropes of productivity—anything to keep our hands moving, to keep going, to keep the conveyer belt in motion. It is no coincidence we refer to mundane tasks as "busywork." Busywork works well for factories, robots, and fascism, but not so great for anyone who's attempting to do something worthwhile with their waking hours.

Being focused, on the other hand, involves attention, awareness, and intentionality. People sometimes mistake my focused time for busyness because complete focus apes many of the same surface characteristics as busy: namely, the majority of my time is occupied.

The difference, then, is I don't commit to a lot of things, but the tasks and people I commit to receive my full attention. Being focused doesn't allow me to get as much accomplished as being busy; thus, the total number of tasks I complete has gone down over the years, although the significance of each undertaking has gone up—way up. This year I'll do only a few things—publish a book, embark on a tour, teach a writing class—but those efforts will receive all of me.

This might not look good on a pie chart next to everyone who's tallying their productivity metrics, but it certainly feels better than being busy just for the sake of being busy.

Sure, sometimes I slip; sometimes I fall back into the busy trap that has engulfed our culture. When I do, I make an effort to notice my slip-up and then course correct until I'm once again focused on only the worthwhile aspects of life. It's a constant battle, but it's one worth fighting.

KILLING TIME
by Joshua Fields Millburn

Somehow I got rid of time without even noticing.

Last week I was walking the city streets, the scorching sun overhead, and someone stopped me and asked me for the time. I looked up at the sky and responded with two words: "It's daytime."

I didn't mean for my answer to sound glib or off-putting, but it was the only answer I had. I didn't have my phone with me, and I don't own a watch. Truly, I had no idea what time it was.

Throughout my minimalist journey, I've learned a lot about change, often forcing myself to grow by way of experimentation: I stopped buying junk, I got rid of my TV, I killed the Internet at home, I stopped using a dishwasher, I started questioning my possessions, I donated 90% of my stuff, I left corporate America, I got into the best shape of my life, I got rid of goals, and I started contributing to other people.

I did many of these things to test my limits, to grow as an individual, but I wrote about these experiences to show people changes are possible—and often easier than we think.

Sometimes, however, my changes are accidental, as was the change I noticed most recently: these days I rarely keep track of time.

Over time, I got rid of time.

I sold my watches.
I donated all my clocks.
I removed the clock from my computer.
I got rid of my microwave, which had a clock.
I tossed my alarm clock (I use my phone).

Now my apartment has no clocks. The only clock that remains is the one on my phone, which I usually leave in a separate room if I'm home, and I often leave at home when I'm away. There is a clock in my car, but it's intentionally set to the incorrect time so I can't rely on it.

Now I wake when I want to wake, write when I want to write, exercise when I want to exercise, eat when I want to eat, and live life every minute of every day, irrespective of time.

I realize this time-free approach isn't practical for many people, but maybe it still has a practical application for everyone: maybe you can take one day each month (or even one day a week) and kill the time.

Do we really need a watch *and* a phone with a clock?

Do we really need clocks in every room of our homes?

Without time, it is easier to focus on the task at hand. If I'm spending time with a friend, we can closely listen to each other and not worry about the time. If writing, get lost in the act of writing. If exercising, focus on the specific exercise. And so forth.

Do you think you would be more focused—and perhaps enjoy your days more—if you were less constricted by time?

It's at least worth thinking about, isn't it?

YOUR OWN ADVICE IS THE HARDEST PILL

Giving advice is pretty easy: Anyone can give advice. Anyone can make recommendations. Anyone can tell you what to do. Just because someone spouts their opinion, though, doesn't mean it's the correct advice for you.

It's often easy to take advice from other people when they are dishing it out. Having relationship trouble? We typically ask a friend for advice. Having a conflict with a co-worker? We ask another co-worker for advice. Having money problems? You get the idea.

Sometimes, all we have to do is look in the mirror and ask ourselves for advice. Who knows you better than you? Nobody is more aware of your situation. Nobody is more familiar with every scenario and potential outcome.

So why do we turn to others so often? Because it's easy. If someone tells us what to do, we don't have to think.

Coincidentally (or not-so-coincidentally), this is also how fascism works: someone else makes the decisions for you.

Or sometimes we ask other people for advice to reaffirm our own—but other people rarely have the same stake in the outcome, which makes their opinion less valid than our own.

It's okay to ask others for advice—sometimes it's great to have a fresh pair of eyes—but remember: it is you who must live with your decisions.

THE RIGHT PATH, WRONG PATH, LEFT PATH, AND NO PATH

Whenever we fail to make a decision, we fail to grow.

As we approach each of life's proverbial forks in the road, we are not faced merely with two potential courses of action; rather, as many as four choices appear in front of us at each fork.

The right path. Often the correct decision is glaring: the right path is illuminated, clear for miles, obvious to everyone. Whenever this is the case, seize the opportunity —take the right path.

The wrong path. There are some paths that are blatantly incorrect, filled with obstacles and venomous creatures lurking about. Avoid these routes, even when they appear to be beautiful, tantalizing, or easy.

The left path. Sometimes the fork presents two equally viable options: the right path is right, but so is the left—or maybe you cannot tell which path is correct. In these instances it is most important to simply pick either path, using all available relevant information, and keep moving forward. Even if we pick the wrong path, we grow from the failure.

No path. When we are faced with two unknown paths—left and right—we often freeze with indecision, stuck in our decision-making paralysis. This is the worst option of all: not deciding is always a bad decision.

THE END IS RIGHT PAST THE HORIZON

Every person has dreams and desires. Many of us believe achieving these dreams will bring us satisfaction, fulfillment, or contentment.

You can reach your dreams and feel fulfilled; you can accomplish everything you desire and become satisfied.

But only for a short while.

Accomplishment is transitory. What's impressive and exciting today is easy—infantile—tomorrow. Millions of examples illustrate this point: tying your shoe for the first time, dribbling a basketball between your legs, an awkward first kiss, etc., etc. Over time, people grow, and with growth comes grace, poise, and—most importantly—the responsibility to keep growing.

Growth is an elusive horizon: you can travel toward it, but

you'll never "get there": there will always be a new horizon to venture toward. Similarly, we should all work toward an *ideal* for every area of our lives, an ideal body, an ideal diet, ideal relationships, an ideal work environment, and so forth. While doing this, we must realize we'll never reach our *ideal*; if we do, it won't be our ideal situation for long, because human beings yearn to grow, and that which is ideal today likely won't be ideal tomorrow.

You can achieve and accomplish whatever you desire, but the key to lasting happiness is continued growth. Keep going, keep moving forward, keep heading toward the horizon: you'll never get there, but that's okay.

WHAT IS MY OUTCOME?
by Joshua Fields Millburn

It is not ambition that sets a man apart: it is the distance he is prepared to go.

I've accomplished a lot in my 31 years on this earth—not because I've had the most ambitious ambitions in the world, and certainly not because I'm smarter or more skilled or better acclimated than the next guy, but because I'm willing to keep going, to keep taking action, to keep moving forward when many other men would give up, give in, or give out. When I'm tired and uninspired, that's when I know I must shake the dust, right myself, and advance.

This type of laudable work ethic doesn't come naturally. It didn't for me, at least. Rather, it's a formula, and it works 100% of the time it's applied.

These days I avoid goals in favor of directions, but that doesn't mean I don't have a recipe for moving forward. The way I see it, you must be willing to ask yourself four questions if you want to accomplish anything. If you do this enough, as I have, it becomes habitual and you begin to do it with everything—literally *everything*—from conversations with co-workers to massive long-term goals.

Question 1: What is my outcome?

This should be an obvious first question in any endeavor. So obvious we usually forget to ask it—we skip ahead to questions three and four, and we end up wondering why we're spinning our wheels.

Another way to ask this question is to ask yourself: *What do I want to happen?* Do I want to lose weight? Do I want to stop fighting with my significant other? Do I want to make a billion dollars? Before you can move forward, you must have a vision of what you want: without a vision, people perish.

Question 2: Why do I want this outcome?

This is the most important of the four questions. So important you won't find satisfaction unless you can adequately answer this question with a high level of detail. Another way to ask it is to ask yourself: *What is the purpose of my outcome?* This question is the *why* behind the *what* —the purpose behind the outcome.

Your purpose gives you the leverage you need to keep going, especially when you reach a roadblock. Without this leverage, it's easy to get excited about a new idea, but quickly fall flat on your face because you no longer know why you wanted your outcome in the first place (i.e., you'll lose interest). You might have that initial ambition, but you must also find enough leverage to take you the distance.

Sometimes we *want* a specific outcome, not knowing *why* we desire that outcome. Perhaps you *want* to make a billion dollars. OK, fine, but *why* do you want to make a billion dollars? "So I can feel secure," you might say. OK, but can't you feel secure without earning a billion dollars? Of course you can. So your real outcome in this case isn't to earn a bunch of money: your outcome is to feel secure. There's nothing wrong with earning money, but you needn't rake in an exorbitant, arbitrary sum to make you feel secure.

To put it simply, you must be willing to change your outcome so you have a good enough reason to see it through.

Question 3: What actions must I take?

Once you know your outcome and why you want your outcome, you must take action. At first, it is important to take massive action, to give you the initial momentum you need to move forward. Then you must be willing to take ongoing, consistent actions until you reach your desired outcome. There's no avoiding this step: we all must take action.

Another way to frame this question is to ask yourself: *What is my strategy?* Remember, *Strategy* is just a fancy way to say *Recipe*. Once you have a recipe, you can use it time and time again to get the same result.

Question 4: Is this working?

Now you know *what* you want, *why* you want it, and you have a *strategy* to get there. Great! You're ahead of 90% of the population. This final question is crucial, though.

If you take massive action and are fortunate enough to achieve your outcome right away, then the answer is simple: *yes, my strategy is working.* If you don't reach your desired outcome, then you must be willing to change your strategy. As long as you have a strong enough purpose, you'll be willing to change your approach until you get your desired outcome—even if it means testing a thousand different routes before you reach your destination. If you're not getting what you want, change is a must. After all, doing the same thing repeatedly and expecting a different result is the definition of insanity.

When I was a kid, my mother used to say, *If at first you don't succeed, try, try again.* Unfortunately, as adults, we tend to do the opposite: we get discouraged or embarrassed or ashamed when our recipe doesn't work, and although we make it 90% of the way to our outcome, we give up. We quit. We fall short of the finish line. What's strange is these feelings of discouragement and embarrassment are completely mental. If we fail, we look around and hope no one noticed, and we vow to never do it again. Big mistake.

We must fail. We must figure out what doesn't work so we can figure out what does. Children already know this part of the formula: every child fails hundreds of times before she is able to walk. But what does the child do? Does she try a handful of times and then cower in embarrassment after failing? No, she continually changes her strategy, she keeps trying until she gets it right. That's what all kids do. And now nearly every person in the world can walk.

We don't need goals to live a compelling, meaningful, purpose-driven life, and we certainly don't need goals to make us happy. If you're not getting what you want, though, it's a good idea to ask yourself these four questions. They might help you clear the clutter obstructing your path.

Thankfully, this formula doesn't work only for large goals: it works for any situation in your life. For example, if you get into an argument with a loved one, ask yourself these same four questions. You'll quickly discover your desired outcome isn't to *argue*—the outcome you want is something else. Once you uncover your true outcome and its purpose, you can develop a strategy to get what you want, re-evaluating your actions until you reach your outcome.

The same goes for every aspect of life: health, relationships, passion, growth, contribution. If you ask these four questions constantly, you'll uncover myriad revelations about yourself, and you'll accomplish more than you ever thought possible.

(Essay inspired by Anthony Robbins's Ultimate Success Formula.)

WWJD: WHAT WOULD JOSHUA DO?
by Joshua Fields Millburn

Recently, a friend of mine stood in her local grocer's checkout line, fumbling with her wallet's zipper, preparing to make an impulse purchase. But then, suspended in the queue, she was given time to question the item she was about to buy. She pondered the item carefully and asked herself a question: *What would Joshua do?*

If I were there in her shoes, would I make this purchase? *No*, she thought, and promptly returned the item to the shelf.

When she told me about her experience, she joked she should buy one of those *WWJD?* bracelets—the ones so popular in the 90s—to help her avoid compulsory consumption. I laughed, but then I realized I, too, could benefit from making more frequent use of this question—and so could others.

I don't expect, or even want, anyone to walk around asking themselves, *What would Joshua do?* Please don't. At least not aloud. Rather, it's a question *I* should ask myself: *What would the best version of me do in this situation?* Likewise, what would the best version of you do? What would Chris do? What would Katie do? What would your best self do?

Would the best version of me put off writing until tomorrow? Would the best version of you sleep an extra hour and skip the gym? Would the best version of me eat the frosted donut? Would the best version of you lie to your boss? Would the best version of me procrastinate, buy things I don't need, or ignore a friend in need?

Perhaps this question, when employed habitually, can help us change our priorities. It's certainly a question worth asking.

THE RULES WE LIVE BY
by Ryan Nicodemus

I had this friend in high school whose parents had all these strict rules—rules that seemed crazy to me as a teenager.

For example, if she left her clothes on the floor for longer than a day, her mom would throw them away.

Sounds overly strict, doesn't it? Maybe it was, but she didn't leave clothes on the floor after the first time her favorite jeans hit the trash can.

What if we did the same thing with our lives? What if we held ourselves accountable with our rules?

Our lives are nothing but rules anyway. Unfortunately, most of our rules are disempowering: If I make a million dollars, then I can be happy. If I get this promotion, then I'll work harder. If someone doesn't like me, then I'm going to feel hurt. Too often our rules are just debilitating if-then statements.

It's time to make some new rules. Today. Empowering rules —rules that will help us grow.

New rules: If I wake up today, then I'll be happy. If I exercise today, then I'll feel more confident. If I spend focused time with loved ones today, then I'm contributing in a meaningful way. If I step outside my comfort zone today, then I will grow.

The key, though, is sticking to your rules no matter what. Rain, hail, sleet, or snow, you must adhere to the rules you create. As long as your rules are empowering, you'll be glad you did.

DIRECTION
by Joshua Fields Millburn

People have all sorts of clever words to describe what they want to do: Objective. Target. Plan. Endgame. Outcome. Goal.

If you know me, then you know I was The Goal Guy when I was in the corporate world. I had financial goals, health goals, sales goals, vacation goals, even consumer-purchase goals (I shit you not). I had spreadsheets of goals, precisely tracking and measuring and readjusting my plans accordingly.

These days, life is different, and I no longer have goals. Instead of an arbitrary target, I prefer to have a *direction* in which I travel. If you're searching for a sunrise, it's important to be headed east; for a sunset, west.

I do, however, believe there was a time in my life when goals were direly important: when I was in a hole and needed to get out. Truth be told, most of my goals were ridiculous or irrelevant (purchasing and accumulation goals), but a few of my goals helped immensely (getting out of debt and losing 70-80 pounds).

I liken these latter goals to escaping a crater in the middle of the desert. When I was fat and up to my eyeballs in debt, lingering in that bowl-shaped cavity beneath the ground, my goal was to break free from the sun-scorched basin and find the earth's surface. I couldn't even fathom a direction from down there—I simply needed to get out of the hole, and my goals helped me do that. (By the way, I don't want to give too much credit to the goals, since it was actually my consistent actions over time that got me out of those fat and debt craters, not the goals themselves.)

Once I found the surface, though, I no longer needed goals: I simply needed to look around and pick a direction in which to travel. It was Lao Tzu who once said, "a good traveler has no fixed plans and is not intent on arriving."

For me, there were mountains to the west, flat plains to the east, sand dunes to the south, and whispering-pine forests to the north, all blanketed by the complete sum of endless blue heavens above. If I wanted to be on the mountain, I'd travel west. If I wanted to get lost in the forest, I'd head north. And so on.

The nice thing about choosing a direction is you never know what you're going to get: You might head west in search of the mountains on the horizon, but along the way find a beautiful river instead. You might traverse the sand dunes, only to find a village a few miles from the crater. You never know what's around the bend.

Once I got out of my craters, I didn't need goals to enjoy my life: my daily habits help me do that.

I discovered sometimes it's okay to wander in the direction of your choice. If you get lost, so what; would that be so bad? Once you're out of the crater, you simply need to stay out of other craters. You can always change your direction if you're unhappy.

MOVING BEYOND GOALS
by Joshua Fields Millburn

You can't manage what you don't measure—this was the corporate mantra by which I lived for a long time. And it's total bullshit.

We used to measure everything at my old job: There were 29 metrics for which we were responsible every single day (even on weekends). There was morning reporting, 3 p.m. updates, 6 p.m. updates, and end-of-day reporting.

I was consumed by numbers. After a while, I even started dreaming in spreadsheet format.

Then I realized something: it didn't really matter. The goals were never as powerful as someone's internal motivations.

People work hard for two reasons: they are externally inspired, or they are internally motivated. Sometimes it's a combination of both.

Some people can be momentarily inspired by goal

attainment, but that kind of inspiration is impermanent, and it doesn't last beyond the goal itself.

Conversely, intrinsic motivation—such as the desire to grow or contribute—carries on long after the goal is met. It often carries on in perpetuity. External inspiration can be the trigger, but internal motivation is what fuels someone's desire. When you discover your true motivation, you don't need an arbitrary goal.

Goals are for the unmotivated. This is one of the reasons I got rid of mine—so I could focus on what's important, so I could focus on living a life centered around health, relationships, passion, growth, and contribution. I don't need goals to focus on these aspects of my life, because I'm already motivated by these values. Having goals for these things would be irrelevant, I simply need to live my life in accordance with these principles.

THE DISCOMFORT ZONE

You know that dream when you're buck naked at school? Terrifying, isn't it? Everything's unsheltered, out in the open, nude—a nakedness we're thankful to wake from and ease back into our world of comfort and safety.

We often feel an underlying trepidation whenever we do something new, something that makes us feel exposed.

Joshua notices this trepidation with his writing students whenever he asks them to do activities that're outside their comfort zone: when he asks them to tell a stranger about their passion for writing, or when he asks them to write an essay or story that other classmates might read.

Likewise, when Ryan asks the people he mentors to publicly proclaim their goals or to find an accountability partner, these proteges often wince with foreboding. At first, at least.

We refer to this uneasy consternation as "stepping into your Discomfort Zone." We want these people—people we truly care about—to feel temporarily naked: when you're naked, you're most vulnerable, and when you're vulnerable, that's when radical growth happens.

Next time you feel naked, next time you feel defenseless, know you're simply operating from your Discomfort Zone, a place from which you'll experience growth as long as you're willing to sit with your vulnerability long enough to grow.

KILLING THE INTERNET AT HOME
by Joshua Fields Millburn

Earlier this year I made the conscious decision to remove all Internet service from my home. It ended up being the best productivity decision I've ever made.

I was not content with the time I was wasting—I felt I could do more purposeful things with my time than spend it on the Internet.

This doesn't mean I think the Internet is evil, bad, or wrong

—it's not. The Internet is an amazing tool, one that changed my life for the better.

But you run a popular website, how could you possibly go without Internet service at home?

My answer is easy: I plan my Internet use. I don't do so in a regimented way—it's not like I say, "OK, I'll be on Twitter from 2 p.m. to 4 p.m. next Thursday." If I see something I want to research on the Internet, I write it down and use that list when I have Internet access.

Now I'm forced to leave the house to access the Internet. I'll go to the office, the library, the coffee shop, or some other place with free public Wi-Fi, and I'll grab a cup of coffee or something to eat and work on all the stuff I need to do online (publish writing, check email, read blogs, get on goofy websites, etc.). Additionally, because I'm out of the house and there are people around, I meet new people.

But you're a writer, Joshua, and that's why it made sense for you! I need the Internet for homework/work-work/Netflix/ online dating/online gaming/updating my Facebook status/ playing Farmville/surfing eBay for shit I don't need/stalking my high school boyfriend/etc./etc.

You probably don't, and maybe it's time to look in the mirror and be honest with yourself.

I was able to reclaim the time I once wasted. No longer am I taking unconscious breaks from my life to watch YouTube videos, movie trailers, or to look at funny pictures on some random site.

Now when I'm on the Internet, it has a purpose—it is a tool I use to enhance my life. Sure, sometimes I log on to watch some funny videos or laugh at memes, but I go to the Internet with the intention of doing these things.

Whenever I'm on the Internet now, I use it in a deliberate way, in a way that benefits me and my life, a way that adds value.

When I got rid of the Internet at home, I did it mostly so I could focus on writing without distractions—but I found so many extra benefits since I got rid of the Internet:

My time at home is more peaceful now, as if my home is a sanctuary.

I have more time to read.
I have more time to write.
I have more time to think.
I have more time for friends.
I have more time to exercise.
I have more time to walk.
I am less distracted.
I am less stressed.
My thoughts are clearer and less fragmented.
I no longer crave the Internet like I once did.
My mind is more focused on important things.
I don't have a monthly Internet bill.

Here are some of my tips to help you use the Internet in a deliberate, more productive way (this is what I do): Check email no more than once a day. Keep a list of what you want to do on the Internet (watch videos, listen to songs, stuff you want to read, etc.). Subscribe to your favorite websites and blogs via email, so they come directly to your inbox. Give yourself one or two hours per week to just goof-off on the Internet (make it a treat, like that piece of candy).

That's great for you, Joshua, but I could never do it!

Don't kill your Internet, then, but do this:

Embark on a 30-day trial. Take your modem and get it out of the house—take it to work, take it to a friend's house, or do whatever you need to do get it out of the house for 30 days—just make sure you don't have access to it.

You will hate it at first. You'll want to get online to do something stupid and you won't be able to. Then you'll want to get online to do something "important," but you won't be able to do that, either. It's like quitting smoking: you'll have a craving to get online, and it will take a while to get rid of that craving (that's why I recommend at least 30 days).

You will be frustrated at first—very, very frustrated at times —but you will live, and your life will be better without it: you will be able to do more worthwhile things, and you will remove some of the discontent from your life. If not, you can always go back.

What do you have to lose? Better yet—what do you have to gain?

LETTING GO OF VACATION PHOTOS
by Joshua Fields Millburn

Imagine yourself reaching for your camera-phone as the sun sets beneath billowing clouds, a smear of pale pink on the horizon. You take a picture. And then another. And then another.

We all want to capture the moment. We desire to preserve it forever, salvaging the beauty of everything we see. So we grab our cellphones, our iPads, our digital cameras, and *SNAP!* We take a few photos to safeguard our memories.

Harmless, right? I mean, look around—everyone's doing it. You can't go to a monument, a concert, or even a sunset without scads of pedestrians fiddling with their electronics, trying to save and share the experience.

There seems to be two problems with this incessant picture-taking behavior, and I have been an accomplice to said problem for way too long.

First, by fumbling around with my device, looking for the best angle and filter, snapping the picture, viewing the picture, and then often retaking the shot in an effort to get the "right" photo, I'm missing the actual moment. My desire to capture the moment actually *ruins* the moment. It makes it less beautiful, less real, and in many ways less photo-worthy.

Second, the "result" is artificial: time doesn't happen in this kind of take-and-retake way. We don't get to re-do the experiences of our lives, and yet we take our pictures as if we can "get it just right." It gives us a false sense of security, a sense we can not only change the moment, but somehow save only its best parts. Yet the best parts exist *because* of the worst parts, not despite them: we cannot enjoy life's mountains without its valleys.

During my last vacation, I avoided reaching for my phone to take pictures. Though I was conscious about this choice, I slipped up a few times. Every beautiful sunset, every Wyoming sky, every rushing Montana river, brought with it the Twitch, an urge to reach for my camera-phone and seize the picturesque setting. I resisted, though, and after an instant of hesitation, I was able to enjoy each event for all its worth—not attempting to put a piece of it in my pocket to save for later. I took it all in—right then, right there—enjoying the experience for what it was: a perfect moment.

Don't get me wrong: I think photography is a beautiful art form. When well-executed, photos are breathtaking. Furthermore, we're a visual culture, so pictures play a large role in the way we communicate. I'm not going to stop taking photos altogether, but I am going to remain more cognizant of my surroundings. I'm going to enjoy the experience first and embrace the impermanence of the moment. And if an unobtrusive opportunity arises to snap a single photo, then I will. Maybe. Or maybe not. It's okay to be on the mountain without proving to everyone else you were there to see it.

PRIME OPTIMIST
by Ryan Nicodemus

I've been excited by exactly one underwear advertisement in my life.

Sometime during my childhood there was a television commercial for underwear embroidered with Optimus Prime—the leader of the good robots, the Autobots—on the Transformers cartoon. It was the most exciting underwear advertisement ever. Whenever the kids in the commercial put on their briefs they transformed into Optimus. Every time that commercial aired I would beg my mom to buy me a pair. I wanted to transform, too.

One day my mother came home with a package of that same, colorful underwear. It was early afternoon and the sun was beaming through the living room windows—not the normal time of day to be changing one's undies, but as soon as she handed me the package I ran to my room, and in no time I was standing in front of the mirror, wearing only my shirt and my new robot-clad drawers, my hands placed proudly on my hips as I awaited my impending transformation. I didn't feel anything except excitement.

After a moment the excitement began to wane. I thought to myself, *Wait, maybe I'm not transforming because my eyes are open*. I squeezed my eyes shut as tight as I could, and my excitement level rose once again. I opened my eyes, but to my dismay all I saw in the mirror was a dorky kid with his hands on his hips, with nothing but Transformer underwear and an old teeshirt on his pudgy body. No metal, no cool transformed parts—just me.

This was my first experience with self-actualization. As it all came crashing down, I realized I wasn't going to transform while standing there in front of the mirror.

Every child grows up with exaggerated hopes and dreams. They grow up with an idea of what they want to become, their ideal self. To adults, childhood dreams—childhood ideals—are cute, but farfetched. Something happens when we become older: at a certain point, we realize simply putting on underwear with pictures of robots isn't going to change us. Worse, as life shapes us, too often the pendulum starts to swing the other way: We start doubting ourselves. We don't give ourselves enough credit. Our hopes and desires become under-exaggerated.

Self-actualization has to do with a person living up to his or her full potential. When Kurt Goldstein talks about self-actualization, he describes it as the ability of an organism to realize its full potential in the present moment. Self-actualization is what drives an organism to live. Kids might not morph into large robots when they change their undergarments, but that doesn't mean they can't transform into something cool over the long haul. As we mature we have the opportunity to grow.

It's easier to grow if we first visualize, as concretely as possible, what we want to grow into. Before we set goals, before we take the first step in the right direction, we must see our full potential through self-actualization. If we don't, we'll keep looking for the quick fix: we'll keep looking to change ourselves by just changing our underwear.

CHAPTER EIGHT || **Health**

HEALTH IS A VEHICLE, NOT A DESTINATION

by Joshua Fields Millburn

We often have a misguided, binary view of personal health. Case in point: a reader took umbrage with a "sign" in our recent essay, "11 Signs You Might Be Broke" (which is featured in the "Finances" chapter of this book). She didn't like what we had written about health, stating, "I'm normally a huge fan [of *The Minimalists*], but this article really annoyed me just because … [it] came across quite judgmental of sick people. … The article might have been better if they'd stuck to ten points."

But, dear reader, health is the most important aspect of the whole article! Without health we have nothing. Although of course "health" is a continuum—it is different for each of us. Personal health is, by definition, *personal.*

The statement in the article—"Unhealthy equals

depression"—does not suggest we should compare our personal health with everyone else's, and it certainly is not a judgment of anyone who's sick; rather, we all want to be in the best possible health given our unique circumstances.

I broke my back while playing basketball in the eighth grade, nineteen years ago, and I still have a broken vertebra today, which, besides being terribly painful, significantly limits my range of motion compared to, say, a gymnast, an athlete, or just your average 33-year-old guy. I can hardly tie my shoes at times.

However, that doesn't mean I shouldn't strive to be as healthy as I can be given my constraints. Health is perspectival, and so if we want to be happy, then we all must strive to be the healthiest versions of ourselves— broken bones, sickness, warts and all. The Internet is filled with shining examples of people with diseases, disabilities, and broken backs who are able to live meaningful lives because they live as healthily as they can according to their individual situations.

When Ryan and I talk about health, we're not talking about vanity muscles, improved statistics, or competing with others. Those are end results—destinations. Health is not a destination: it is a vehicle.

It's unlikely I'll make it to the NBA with my bad back (not to mention my mediocre ball-handling skills), but that doesn't mean I should feel defeated, broke, broken. It means I must take care of the vehicle I have, providing it with regular tune-ups (daily stretching, regular exercise, and occasional chiropractor visits, as well as a good diet, adequate sleep, and daily meditation), which will help me better enjoy the journey ahead.

A MINIMALIST'S THOUGHTS ON DIET
by Joshua Fields Millburn

I hardly get sick anymore. A few years ago, I used to be a meat-'n'-potatoes kind of guy, and I caught a cold several times a year—even when I wasn't sick, I didn't feel great. Actually, I felt like shit most of the time. I weighed appreciably more than I weigh now, I had stomach problems, I was tired and sluggish, and I lacked the energy necessary to live an active, fulfilling life.

Today, my diet is markedly different, and I've never felt more alive. And this is why:

Food. My diet today consists mostly of plants and unprocessed foods. I eat an abundance of vegetables: I'm particularly fond of avocados, spinach, broccoli, and anything green—not because they taste good, but because these foods makes me *feel* outstanding. I also eat fish, nuts, and seeds most days. My ideal meal looks something like this: a bowl containing a small portion of rice, half an avocado, a large piece of grilled salmon, a handful of almonds, and a massive spinach-carrot-cucumber side salad with almond oil and lemon.

Avoid. There are quite a few foods I've drastically reduced —or completely eliminated—from my diet: bread, pasta, sugar, gluten, meat (other than fish), bottom-feeding seafood (lobster, crab, and other garbagemen of the sea), most dairy products, and anything processed or packaged. There are many so-called experts out there—I am *not* one of them—but it was my friend *common sense* who advised me to avoid most of these foods. Think about it: besides humans, do you know of any animals who drink another mammal's breast milk? What other animal eats bread, pasta, or candy bars? Our bodies are not meant to consume this junk (one can make a good argument for eating meat, but I know I feel much better without it, and *feeling better* is my touchstone). *But Joshua, how do you get enough protein, calcium, iron?* How does the world's strongest primate, the gorilla, consume enough of these nutrients? Gorillas eat vegetables and fruit—leaves and bananas (many green vegetables are comprised of 20–45% protein).

Intermittent Fasting. I eat two meals a day (generally no snacks), both consumed within an eight-hour window, usually around 11 a.m. and 6:30 p.m. I fast during the day's remaining sixteen hours (7 p.m. to 11 a.m.), consuming only water, herbal tea, or black coffee during those times. This is much easier than you think. If you want to lose weight, particularly fat, then intermittent fasting will make a drastic difference in your life. And yes, this means I skip breakfast. Visit Martin Berkhan's website, *LeanGains.com*, to learn more about I.F.

Water, Liquids, and Juice. I drink roughly half my bodyweight in ounces of water each day. I weigh 165-ish pounds, so I drink 80–90 ounces of water per day. I'm also fond of drinking a couple powdered green drinks every day for increased vitality (personally, I enjoy Amazing Grass GREENSuperFood). Additionally, I own a masticating juicer and a blender, both of which are great for juicing and blending fresh vegetables and fruits, directly supplying my body with the nutrients I need. I also drink coffee, albeit appreciably less than I used to, as well as herbal tea, but I eliminated cola and all sugary liquids from my diet (including fruit juices, which contain shockingly high amounts of sugar).

Supplements. Although I eat a large quantity of nutrient-rich foods, I find it important to take daily supplements with each meal: multivitamin (comprehensive nutritional health), vitamin B-complex (cardiovascular health), and fish oil (omega-3 fatty acids for heart health). Depending on your diet, these may not be necessary for everyone, but I noticed a considerable difference in my body after two months of these daily supplements.

Exercise. I exercise every day, but I don't spend a ton of time, effort, or focus on it. I do only two things: 1) I walk between three and eight miles each day, allowing me plenty of time to think, breathe, and de-stress as I meander the neighborhoods near my home; and 2) I work out for eighteen minutes (more on that in the following essay). I'm not worried about building vanity muscles—I'm concerned with how I feel. I discovered when I eat and exercise in ways that help me feel good, lean muscles are a nice bonus. You don't have to kill yourself to become fit. My friend, personal trainer Vic Magary, is the fittest guy I know and yet he exercises ten minutes a day. Everyone has 10–20 minutes a day to dedicate to their health, right?

Sleep. Because of diet and exercise, I need less sleep than I used to. Most mornings I awake around 3:30 a.m., after five or six hours of sleep. Some days, however, I sleep later, until 7 a.m. or 8 a.m. I let my body dictate how much sleep

I need, which happens to be far less sleep than just a few years ago. It is important, however, to get as much sleep as your body requires: operating on a deficit is unhealthy.

Stress. We don't *get* stressed, we *do* stressed. If I were to ask you what a stressed person looks like, you'd easily be able to mimic his or her physiology. Frowning, shallow breathing, muscle tensing, etc. Once you become aware of your stressed physiological state, you can change your physiology—the way you move your body—to become unstressed. Nearly everyone feels stressed these days, but I am significantly less stressed than I've ever been, because I make an effort to be aware of my triggers and change my physical movements accordingly. When I feel overwhelmed, I'll change my breathing pattern, I'll take a walk, I'll exercise, I'll look in the mirror with a big grin, or I'll make sure no one's looking and I'll jump up and down like a crazy person—anything to get me out of that stressed state. (These techniques effectively combat depression, anger, and sadness, too.)

Most important, after changing my diet and embracing a healthier lifestyle, I feel amazing.

But Joshua, your diet sounds so boring and unentertaining!

I don't think so, but then again I no longer look at food as entertainment. Food is fuel, nothing more. I can still enjoy a great conversation over a healthy meal with friends—I simply don't let the food be my source of entertainment. I enjoy the food I eat, but I enjoy the rest of my life, too.

Does that mean my exact diet will also work for you? Maybe. But maybe not. There's only one way to know for sure: test it out yourself. You can emulate my diet for ten days and see how it makes you feel, see what aspects work for you. Or try any one aspect for ten days: go without sugar or bread or processed foods, add green drink or fresh juice or daily exercise, and notice the changes. I'm certain you can do anything for ten days. See how those changes make you feel, and then adjust accordingly.

Improving one's health is the foundation of living a meaningful life: without your health, nothing else matters. I don't care what you eat or how you exercise—I'm not looking to convert anyone to my way of eating. I don't care whether you're a vegetarian, a vegan, or a primal-paleo-whatever. None of these labels apply to my own dietary lifestyle, and arguing the particulars is silly anyway. What I do care about is how you feel: I want you to feel great so you can better enjoy your life.

18-MINUTE MINIMALIST EXERCISES

by Joshua Fields Millburn

A few years ago, I couldn't do a single push-up—and I certainly couldn't do a pull-up. I hardly exercised at all; and when I did exercise, it was sporadic: it never lasted more than a few days before I gave up. Sound familiar?

Even after I shed 70 pounds of fat—due mostly to diet—I was in terrible shape. At age 28, I was doughy, flabby, and weak.

Not anymore.

At age 30, I'm in the best shape of my life. I'm in good shape because I've found ways to enjoy exercising; I've found ways to make exercise a daily reward instead of a dreaded task.

I can point to three reasons exercise is now enjoyable.

I do only exercises I enjoy. I don't enjoy running, so I don't do it. I attempted it for six months and discovered it wasn't for me. If you see me running, call the police— someone is chasing me. Instead, I find other ways to do cardio: I walk, I get on the elliptical machine at the gym, I do bodyweight exercises that incorporate cardio.

Exercise relieves stress. Although I enjoy exercising most in the mornings, I love hitting the gym (or the park) in the evenings if I feel tense or stressed. Exercising at the end of a long, stressful day also gives me time in solitude to reflect on what's important.

Variety keeps exercise fresh. When I first started exercising, I used to hit the gym three times per week, which was certainly better than not exercising at all. Then, as I got more serious, I started going to the gym daily. This routine became time-consuming, and doing the same thing over and over eventually caused me to plateau. These days I mix it up: I walk every day, and I still hit the gym occasionally, but the thing that has made the biggest, most noticeable difference has been the variety of daily eighteen-minute bodyweight exercises.

Eighteen minutes?

I know, eighteen minutes sounds like an arbitrary number.

That's because it is. When I started these bodyweight exercises, I didn't have a specific window of time in mind. But I timed myself for a week and discovered that almost every time I hit the park for my exercises, I was worn out within eighteen minutes. Thus, these are my eighteen-minute exercises (all of which you can do in your living room, outdoors, or just about anywhere).

I usually alternate between the following exercises. You can of course pepper in your own favorites. And, yes, these exercises are suitable for men *and* women.

Push-ups. Like I said, a few years ago I couldn't do a single push-up. Eventually, I could do one (after doing modified push-ups for a while). After a while, I could do ten and then 20. Now I can do 50–100. I tend to do three to five sets, resulting in about 200–400 push-ups within my eighteen minutes.

Pull-ups. Two years ago I thought I'd never be able to do a pull-up. Eventually, I learned how to do one. Soon, two, and then four. Now I can do 10–15 in a row. I complete three to four sets, resulting in about 50 pull-ups within my eighteen minutes. I use monkey bars at the park. You can use a pull-up bar at home. A friend of mine uses tree branches. I hated pull-ups because they seemed impossible, but now it's my favorite exercise.

Squats. I just started doing bodyweight squats, and I've already noticed a huge difference. I'm doing only three or four sets of 30 right now, but I'll continue to work my way up—I'll continue to grow.

I don't have a specific routine or plan, I simply take a 30-

second break between sets, bouncing from one exercise to the next. After eighteen minutes, I'm spent. And I feel great afterward. I get that wonderful tired-but-accomplished feeling you get after a great workout. What used to be tedious is now exhilarating.

SIMPLE TRIGGERS
by Joshua Fields Millburn

There's a pull-up bar at the bottom of my stairs.

My writing space is upstairs, so each time I head downstairs I bust out six quick pull-ups: 1, 2, 3, 4, 5, 6. These six take less than 20 seconds, no time at all in the grand scheme of things.

That's not the point, though: the point is each time I go downstairs—on my way to the kitchen, the shower, or the great outdoors—I do some pull-ups. One triggers the other. It's habitual. Now on an average day I sneak in an extra 60-or-so pull-ups.

Every habit has its trigger. Most of the time we don't know our triggers, though, and much of the time we unconsciously trigger *bad* habits: finishing a meal triggers a cigarette, arriving home triggers hours of TV viewing, incessant alcohol consumption triggers arguing with loved ones.

We can, however, change our behaviors. Be it exercise or diet or even flossing our teeth, we can trigger positive habits—using positive triggers. Small triggers create tiny habits that produce huge results over time. The right triggers can flip your life upside down—in a good way.

Descending the stairs is one of my simple triggers. What are some of yours?

THE TASTE OF HEALTH
by Joshua Fields Millburn

It's 2 a.m. and I'm hemming and hacking in a nondescript motel room somewhere in rural Georgia. The heater beneath the room's lone window thrums continuously. It's below freezing outside. Moonlight is sneaking through a crack in the curtains. Ryan is lying in the other bed, snoring lightly, wearing earplugs to shield himself from my latenight coughs. Fortunately, this is my last night fighting this battle.

You see, I never get sick. Well, I never get sick unless I eat junk food, but I never eat junk food. Well, okay, I don't *usually* eat junk food, but I did earlier this month. A lot. And boy oh boy did I pay the price.

My diet is typically pristine. I avoid the bad-food trinity: bread, sugar, and processed foods. Earlier this month, though, I gave in to all three, eating fancy desserts, artisan breads, and specialty ice cream. I figured I could indulge before starting our most recent tour. I was wrong, and I suffered accordingly.

Two days before leaving Montana, The Minimalists were scheduled to deliver the keynote address at TEDx. On the eve of our presentation, though, I developed strep throat and couldn't speak without sounding like a poor imitation of Marlon Brando in the *Godfather*. I was able to pull through, however—the adrenaline (read: fear) of the stage and its bright lights opened my vocal cords for a few necessary minutes.

But, of course, the problems didn't stop there.

As Ryan and I set out on our 2,600-mile trek to Florida, influenza worked its way through my body. Every muscle ached. Misery permeated my existence for days.

But, of course, the problems didn't stop there, either.

As the flu worked its murderous course, a respiratory infection arrived at my motel doorstop, making it hard to breathe. Coughing kept me awake each night, and because the Nyquil was ineffective in muting my midnight coughs, I was grateful for the codeine a Nebraskan doctor prescribed.

But, of course, the problems didn't even stop there.

When I woke after my first decent sleep in over a week, I was covered in hives. Turns out I'm allergic to codeine. I never felt itchier in my life.

The two weeks previous felt protracted: each interview for the book tour, every mile driven, each sleepless night— everything moved slowly. No one should feel bad for me, though: I take full responsibility for my bad choices. I didn't *get* sick; rather, I invited the sickness in. When I established the conditions for a virus to thrive, the virus showed up and hung out. And invited unruly friends.

Thankfully, I recovered by the time we made it to the Sunshine State, and now I'm back on the good-food wagon. No food is worth feeling as nasty as I felt. Nothing tastes as good as being healthy feels.

The decisions we make today are not evanescent: our current decisions, even the small ones, influence our future selves. If we want to feel great tomorrow, we better make the right decisions right now.

CHAPTER NINE || **Relationships**

WALK A MILE IN MY BLISTERS

by *Joshua Fields Millburn*

I am seated on the warm side of floor-to-ceiling windows in a half-empty cafe, a black coffee on the table in front of me. A thick sheet of ice coats the sidewalk outside. Winter clouds hang over everything, the sky the color of a wet hippopotamus. "Graceless," a song by The National, is playing through the establishment's overhead speakers.

Outside, an attractive woman in a peacoat is traversing the icy walkway tentatively, planting each step with great care before planning the next, her arms outstretched and palms flat, as though she's praying for less gravity. Her prayer goes unanswered, though, and with one misplaced step she slips backward. Her arms slice the air violently, reaching for something that isn't there, until her backside connects with the concrete. *Thwap!*

I wince—not because I feel her pain (literally), but because I feel her pain (figuratively). As the woman's rear greeted the pavement, a twinge reverberated throughout my body. I, too, have fallen, so I know what it feels like—or, rather, I know what it feels like to *me*. This is a key difference.

Whenever we pejoratively tell someone to "walk in our shoes," we're simply asking another person to put herself in our position for a moment, to be sympathetic of our circumstance. When we do this, though—when we walk a mile in someone else's shoes—we're still approaching the situation from our own biased perspectives, which still may not allow us to empathize with the person who's loaning her sneakers.

Sympathy and empathy are not the same thing: sympathy *understands* someone's pain, empathy *feels* it. We can never be truly empathetic—we can't completely feel what another person feels—but that doesn't mean we can't try. When we care about another human, we must do our best to approximate their pain, first by understanding, and then by attempting to feel the same thing they feel.

Sympathy is our first step toward empathy. We must wear another person's shoes before we can experience the blisters from their daily trek. By sliding into *your* moccasins, I can better understand what it feels like for *me* to walk in your shoes, even though I'll never wholly understand what it's like for you. I might not feel the weight of your journey, not totally at least, but I'll certainly be closer when I'm donning your footwear.

Sympathetic of what the woman is feeling on the sidewalk outside, I dash out the door to assist. I don't, however, notice the small patch of black ice just beyond the doorway, and *THWAP!* I suffer a similar fate. Both on our asses now, I may not feel the woman's pain, but I feel something close to it. After staring upward, as if the sky is to blame, we share a smile before the woman hops up and helps me off the ground.

MEANINGFUL RELATIONSHIPS
by Joshua Fields Millburn

For many years, I associated with people based on convenience.

The people who were closest to me were the people who were, well, *closest* to me. That is, I spent most of my time with people whose only commonality was proximity: schoolmates, co-workers, acquaintances, networking buddies, etc.

Most of them weren't bad people, but other than location, we had very little in common. We didn't share similar values or beliefs—the bedrocks of any worthwhile relationship. In many cases we didn't even share any common interests.

My life is appreciably different now: I live more deliberately. Accordingly, my relationships are more deliberate, too. Besides two of my closest relationships—Nicodemus and my wonderful former spouse—and a handful of friendships spawned from yesteryear, I've met all my most meaningful relationships online.

That's right: *I've met most of my closest friends on the Internet.* Although weird to read and weird to write, it's the magnificent truth, for good reasons.

People ask me about my relationships all the time, usually with respect to dating or intimate relationships, e.g., "Now that you're a minimalist, do you find the women you date have a problem with your lifestyle?"

My answer: Why the hell would I want to spend significant chunks of time with someone who doesn't share similar values or interests? My lifestyle is predicated on certain principles, and thus my relationships—intimate or otherwise—must align with my personal standards. It's hard to grow with someone if you're both growing in opposite directions.

Because of the Internet, however, you and I are no longer relegated by proximity. We're no longer forced to engage in pointless small talk in an effort to uncover a morsel of commonality. We no longer have to hang out with the guy in the nearby cubicle outside work hours. Instead, we can seek out people with similar values and beliefs.

Most of my newfound relationships have two things in common: we met because of the Internet, and we see the world through similar lenses. That doesn't mean we always agree on everything, nor do we have the same tastes, opinions, or personalities—we're human beings, not robots —but our common interests allow us to forge bonds that are predicated on something much more significant than proximity.

Worthwhile interactions make life more purposeful, they make life worth living. Without them, we'd be forced to experience the world with people who aren't understanding, supportive, or caring—or worse, we'd be forced to encounter the world on our own, completely alone, which doesn't sound like a pleasant proposition—even for an introvert like me.

IT'S COMPLICATED

Don't let Facebook fool you—there is one, and only one, honest relationship status: *It's Complicated.*

Whether you've been married for decades, are recently single, or are involved in some sort of obtuse polyamorous love triangle, it's important to understand relationships—*all* relationships, intimate or otherwise—are inherently complicated. We are human beings, mixed bags of thoughts and emotions and actions, righteous liars and honest cheats, sinners and saints, walking contradictions, both the darkness and the light.

There're going to be times at which you disagree with your partner, argue with your friends, quarrel with the guy in the cubicle next to yours—such is life.

The key, then, is to work through complications with others, to find common ground, to change yourself if you'd like, but never—*ever*—attempt to change someone else. Love, caring, and respect don't work that way. To love someone is to understand them, warts and all. You can provide guidance, but the people you love still have to steer their own boat.

MORE WINS THAN LOSSES
by Ryan Nicodemus

Throughout my twenties, I was an on-again, off-again alcoholic. An on-again, off-again womanizer. An on-again, off-again drug addict. I was a lot of things I'm not proud of, and I still battle with some of my demons.

I'm not perfect. I still lose sometimes. But there's a key difference between Ryan Past and Ryan Present: I win a lot more today.

The person you are today is directly related to the five people you spend the most time with *and* your role models (TOP FIVE ASSOCIATES + ROLE MODELS = YOU). If someone spends the majority of their time with friends at the bar and aspires to live like Snooki from the *Jersey Shore*, then they've made an obvious lifestyle choice.

Sometimes it's not this obvious.

Examine your friends and role models. If they're not in line with who you want to be, then something needs to change.

Then take *massive* action. Once you see what needs to change, change it. Don't sit around and *should* all over yourself. Can't take immediate action? Fine—pick a date when you're able to implement change and stick to it no matter what. Make change a *must*. If you don't take action, your life won't be any different.

Change means avoiding negative relationships. Change means asking friends and family to embrace change with you. Change means breaking out of your comfort zone.

Change means finding new, empowering relationships and role models. It's not easy, but it is rewarding.

What's the difference between action and *massive* action? My mentoring clients ask me this all the time. The difference is that massive action creates a physiological shift. Sitting down and writing out how you need to change is taking action; joining a new group of people to make new friends is taking massive action. If your actions don't move you (literally *move* you) in the direction you want to be, then it's not massive action.

Lastly, realize there is no endgame: once you reach greatness, keep being great. Often, when I would reach *success* (what I used to call *success*), I would use my bad habits as a way to reward myself. I did this with health and exercise. As soon as I saw good (not great) results, I would *reward* myself by slacking off and eating unhealthily. This attitude will destroy your momentum. You don't have to fall back to your old habits; you get to move forward toward better ones.

Keep your head up. I have failed many times, and I still do. The key is to fail less as time goes on.

BUILDING YOUR TRUST MUSCLE
by Joshua Fields Millburn

The most important skill I learned during my dozen years in the corporate world was *trust*.

When I started managing people in my early twenties, I

tried to micromanage their work. The more I tried to be involved in every detail—that is, the more I tried to do their work on my own—the more distrust I showed.

As the years went on, however, I managed more and more employees, hundreds of people, and I was forced to relinquish control.

Every good leader has this skill; I don't know a single great leader who is also a great micromanager.

Trust isn't something that just happens, though—you must develop your trust muscle. To do so one must relinquish control—simply let go.

People will fail: they will let you down—that's inevitable. You can let those failures disappoint you, or you can let them help you grow. One failure isn't the end of the world. Over time, the people who repeatedly succeed will solidify the trust you've placed in them, and the people who consistently fail will lose your trust altogether.

ASKING FRIENDS, FAMILY TO EMBRACE CHANGE

Change isn't easy. More often than not, we don't change because we get in our own way. Other times we don't make a change because we're afraid of what people will think about us, afraid of what they will say about us, afraid they will treat us differently.

Ultimately, we are afraid of rejection.

When we approached minimalism, we realized many of our closest friends and family members were supportive of the changes we wanted to make. And in other cases, many of them were neutral bystanders, ambivalent to the simplification going on around us.

In some instances, some of the people closest to us didn't approve of our new paths. Some of these people mistook the journey on which we were embarking as a direct attack on *their* way of life, as if by questioning our lives we were also questioning their lives by proxy. Clearly this was not our intent. Our journey involved questioning our lives, not theirs. We were simply looking for happiness, using minimalism as a tool to search for deeper meaning.

Yet, some people thought the changes we were making were silly, stupid, and even crazy (literally). We had worked hard for more than a decade to accumulate all these nice material possessions, big houses, fancy cars, "important" job titles, and the American Dream, all of which was supposed to make us happy, right?

When the consumerist, over-indulgent lives we were leading didn't make us happy, there had to be something wrong with *us*. At least that's what the naysayers said: Maybe Joshua & Ryan went crazy. Maybe they are experiencing a *mid*-midlife crisis. Maybe they joined a cult (someone actually accused us of joining a cult, likening minimalism to Jonestown and Branch Davidian).

We had to explain a few things to these naysayers:

It's not you, it's me. We've all heard this line before. It has been parodied a thousand times, but there is a profound truth to be discovered here. We weren't questioning anyone else's lifestyle but our own. Many people weren't happy with their own situations, and they aspired to be like us because they thought we "had it figured out." We didn't have it figured out, though, and that frustrated some people because we were who they wanted to emulate: we had the material possessions, the salaries, the awards, the facade of power, the fast-track to corporate success. We looked around us, though, and realized most of the people above us, people several rungs higher on the corporate ladder, weren't happy, either—they were far less happy than we were. What were we supposed to do—keep working exceptionally hard and aspire to continue to be unhappy? It's alright to tell naysayers you're making changes in your life so you can be happy. Better yet, you can do what we did and ask those naysayers a question: "You want me to be happy, don't you?"

Circumstances change. If our 28-year-old selves could have time-traveled back to 1999 to tell our eighteen-year-old selves about everything we were going to "accomplish" over the next decade, the teenage Joshua & Ryan would have been elated. *You mean I'm going to have this, that, and this? You mean I'll be able to afford this?* The happiness would have soon faded, though, and by 28 (or perhaps much sooner) an overwhelming cloak of discontent would have enveloped our lives. That's because circumstances change. Thus, *we* must change: we must continue to evolve and grow if we expect to be happy. What adds value to your life today, may not add value to your life tomorrow.

You, too, can change. Minimalism may not be the answer for you. If you're not happy, though, you, too, can build your change muscle and, over time, change your circumstances. There are many paths to happiness. Minimalism simply allowed us to clear the clutter from our paths so we could find that happiness sooner.

Show people the benefits. As we journeyed farther down our paths, many of the naysayers jumped on board. Not because we asked them to—we've never asked anyone to embrace minimalism—but because they saw the happiness we'd welcomed into our lives. They saw that for the first time in our adult lives we were truly excited, joyous, and content with who we were. They saw that perhaps we *didn't* have it figured out before, and maybe we didn't have it figured out now, but we certainly appeared to be on the right track. The actions alone didn't convince them, but once they saw the benefits, they better understood the changes we'd undergone.

There were, however, some relationships we had to get rid of. It wasn't easy, but certain people—friends and family—weren't adding value to our lives, they were sources of negativity, and they prevented us from growing. We treated this option as a last resort, but it's important to know that, as we grow, even our relationships can change. Today, many of our old friends are still our friends—while others are not—but we've also established new, empowering relationships that encourage our constant growth and help us enjoy what we contribute to the relationship.

LETTING GO OF SHITTY RELATIONSHIPS

Some relationships are particularly pernicious. We often develop relationships out of convenience, without considering the traits necessary to build a successful bond with another person—important traits like unwavering support, shared trust, and loving encouragement.

When a relationship is birthed out of proximity or chemistry alone, it is bound to fail. We need more than a person's physical presence to maintain a meaningful connection, but we routinely keep people around simply because they're already *around*.

It's easy to develop a connection with a co-worker, schoolmate, or someone who's always there—even when they're not adding any real value to our lives. It's even easier to stay in those relationships: old relationships are comfortable, and starting new relationships is difficult—it requires work. Anything worth holding on to does.

We've all held on to someone who didn't deserve to be there, and most of us still have someone in our lives who continually drains us: Someone who doesn't add value. Someone who isn't supportive. Someone who takes and takes and takes without giving back to the relationship. Someone who contributes very little and prevents us from growing. Someone who constantly plays the victim.

Victims become victimizers, though, and these people are dangerous: They keep us from feeling fulfilled. They keep us from living purpose-driven lives. Over time, these negative relationships become part of our identity—they define us, they become *who we are*.

Fortunately, this needn't be the case: several actions can be taken to rid ourselves of negative relationships.

First, you can attempt to fix the relationship. This is obviously the preferable solution (albeit not always possible or worthwhile). People change over time, and so do relationships. You can change how your relationship works —be it marriage, friendship, or family—without completely ditching the relationship.

Sit down with the person who's draining the vitality from your life and explain to them what must change in order for your relationship to work. Explain you need them to be more supportive, you need them to participate in your growth, and they are important to you, but the relationship in its current state does not make you happy. Explain you're not attempting to change them as a person: you simply want to change how your relationship works.

Finally, ask them what they'd like to change about the relationship. Ask them how you can add more value. Listen attentively, act accordingly.

If you're unable to change the relationship, end it. This is difficult, but it applies to any relationship: family, friends, lovers, co-workers, acquaintances. If someone is only draining your life, it's perfectly acceptable to tell them: "This relationship is no longer right for me, so I must end it —I must move on."

It's okay to move on. You owe it to yourself to move on. You owe it to yourself to be happy in your relationships. You are in control.

Moving on is sometimes the only way to develop new, empowering relationships. Starting anew, empty-handed and full-hearted, you can build fresher, stronger, more supportive relationships—important relationships that allow you to have fun, be happy, and to contribute beyond yourself. These are the relationships we all need.

It's also important to do your part. You, too, must add value to the relationship. Not by buying gifts or commoditizing your love, but by showing up every day and rigorously exhibiting how much you care, demonstrating your love through consistent actions, continually going out of your way to help the other person grow.

Both people must do their part to grow the relationship—only then will both of you be satisfied with the relationship you've built.

GOODBYE FAKE FRIENDS
by Joshua Fields Millburn

Dear fake friends from my past:

When I walked away from a successful career several years ago, you thought I was crazy. Even crazier when I said I wanted to cultivate my passion, to pursue my dream—writing. It's all right, there's no need to deny it now. Save your apologies; I'm not looking for one.

Scores of you, my so-called friends, talked behind my back. The grapevine is not self-contained, so, yes, the terrible things you said got back to me. You said I was dumb, out of touch, too idealistic. You gossiped, told people I'd lost my mind. I was an idiot, you said. I'd be broke and alone in no time.

Truth be told, it was upsetting—gut-wrenching and heartrending—to hear the vitriol that was spewed. I thought you were different. I thought we were different. I thought we were friends.

You, my lip-service friends, told me it was impossible. If people could make a living from their passions, you said, then everyone would be doing it. I was making a mistake, a horrible decision. I'd regret giving up the money, the status, the ostensible success. My plan would never work out.

It's evident now you were merely projecting your fears, hoping I would fail so your flawed idea of success would remain unblemished.

Well, guess what: I don't regret my change in lifestyle. Everything did work out—and then some. My life is better now than it ever was in that corner office. Substantially better. Be it money, passion, health, my life has improved exponentially. Even my friends have changed for the better.

You see, my real friends, although they may've not fully understood my decision at the time, they supported me through the transition. Real support. They encouraged me, cheered me on, offered help when I needed it. In truth, it took this type of radical change to understand who my real friends were—and who was just hanging on because I had an impressive job title or the shiny things they wanted.

Without the facade of a big paycheck or an oversized house, I made new friends, people whose interests, values, and beliefs align with mine. Wonderful people who care about me for me, not what's printed on my business card.

So I guess this is goodbye, fake friends of old. I'm walking away, for good, and you likely won't be able to catch up. But first, I'd like to thank you for teaching me one of life's most important lessons:

You can't change the people around you, but you can change the people around you.

KNOW THY NEIGHBOR
by Ryan Nicodemus

Do you know your neighbors? I mean, do you really *know* your neighbors?

I lived in a condo development in which there were roughly 80 units, and I really didn't know any of the people living there other than a few of their names and faces. I didn't value the relationships, or potential relationships.

When I first moved into the neighborhood, I looked at the situation like any other single bachelor—it was an opportunity to live in a nice place virtually maintenance-free. With a busy life, I enjoyed the thought of not spending hours on upkeep every week, doing maintenance work that people who own houses do regularly.

Or so I thought.

After the first few months of living there, I realized there were a plethora of issues with the condo association. They hardly did anything around the place other than mow the grass and keep up on small odds and ends (roof leaks, siding repairs, etc.). With the tough economic times they had not been able to add much value to the property.

At one point I was solicited by several board members to impeach other members on the board. I was asked to pick sides and support the election of a new board. Since I didn't know any of my neighbors it was hard to choose which side was right, and it was difficult to decipher who was right and who was wrong—it felt like everyone was being negative (including myself).

After just a year of living there I wanted to leave because of this, and after adopting a minimalist lifestyle I especially wanted out of there, realizing I had this gigantic place all to myself. It was overwhelming.

I spent many days frustrated and blamed the board for the bickering and inability to manage the budget. This was *their fault*, not mine. I fell into this "why me" stage, which only exacerbated my frustration.

One of my neighbors (who was on the board) sent out an email asking for everyone in the community to pitch in and volunteer to do some upkeep around the community—to make the place a little nicer and increase morale. My first thought when I saw this email was, "Why do I pay condo dues if I have to do the upkeep myself?" Then I realized that this attitude toward the board, and the "why me" attitude, was only worsening the situation. So I did the opposite of what I wanted to do: I replied and said I would help.

When the workday rolled around there were six owners including myself (out of roughly 80) who showed up to help. I did not let this discourage me, because, again, I was sick of fueling my frustration. I worked my ass off and did what needed to be done for the day.

As we worked, I got to know my five neighbors and I realized they were just as frustrated as me. I also developed a good relationship with the board member who arranged the community workday. I felt better about the changes he was trying to make. It took the board about five years to sink the association, and after talking with him, I realized it was probably going to take a few years to repair the damage.

Until I actually got to know my neighbors that day I honestly thought everyone was out for themselves (which may still be the case with some of them), but they were just like me. After we all spent the day with each other, we felt much closer and formed a bond that was beneficial to our entire community.

7 WAYS TO MAKE CONVERSATIONS MEANINGFUL USING MINIMALISM

Our relationships are one of the most important aspects of living a good life. Conversing with a close friend can be one of the most intimate experiences we have. Yet we often don't value these conversations like we should: we don't pay enough attention to the important people around us.

Just like we use minimalism to get rid of excess stuff in favor of essential things, we can use it to rid ourselves of superfluous conversations in favor of essential ones. Consider these seven actions:

1. **Make your words count**. There is no need to count your words, just make sure they count. Be sure your words add value to your conversations. It is important to be aware of *what* you are saying and, more important, *why* you are saying it.

2. **Expand your vocabulary**. An extensive vocabulary allows us to be more precise, and precision allows us to better convey what we mean in a short span.

3. **Be succinct**. Brevity is the soul of wit.

4. **Avoid unnecessary conversations**. Our words become sloppy when we are forced to partake in a multitude of unnecessary conversations each day. Many of these conversations can be avoided or radically attenuated. Can you think of more than one conversation you could have avoided or shortened yesterday? What could you have done to avoid that conversation?

5. **Converse more with loved ones**. The people who really matter in your life—your friends, family, and loved ones—deserve quality conversation from you. By ridding yourself of unnecessary conversations, you can allocate more time to converse with your loved ones and establish deeper connections.

6. **Listen more than you talk**. Listening—honest, attentive listening—is not easy, and it doesn't come naturally to most; thus, we must make an effort to listen while engaged in conversation.

7. **Ask and listen**. An easy way to be an engaged listener is to ask and listen. This allows you to actively participate in the listening process by asking interesting questions and allowing the other person to respond uninterrupted.

YOU DON'T HAVE TO EXPLAIN YOURSELF

We seem to be explaining ourselves at every turn.

But I only did it because…
And I was just trying to…
No, no, no, what I *meant* was…
Wait! Let me explain!

You probably spend a considerable amount of time explaining yourself, justifying your actions to others as though you were in a court of law.

The people who require an explanation probably won't understand you anyway—you can't control what they think.

The people who *really* understand you—the important people closest to you—don't need any explanation at all. They already *get* you.

Here's a simple solution: *stop explaining yourself.*

If you want to explain yourself, go ahead, it's okay to do so. Just don't feel obligated to—you don't have to waste your time.

ENDING THE TYRANNY OF COOL
by Joshua Fields Millburn

Not so long ago, I wanted to be cool.

Steve McQueen cool. Coca-cola-advertisement cool. New-car-smell cool.

Being cool was important to me—it mattered. I had to have the perfect clothes with the right logos. I had to have my shiny Lexus with the tan leather interior and in-dash navigation system. I had to have stainless steel appliances, hardwood floors, modern furniture, and all the trappings propagated by our media-soaked culture.

I was trapped by the tyranny of cool.

If I bought the perfect clothes, then everything would be right, right?

If I drove the perfect car, then everyone would respect me, right?

If I had the right furniture, then I would be happy, right?

I laugh at myself now, but those things were so important to me once upon a time (not too long ago).

Those things forced me to continue to work a job—and not pursue my passions—so I could buy more and more stuff. If I bought more stuff, I'd be more cool, right?

Three separate things made me realize how ridiculous *being cool* really was. These three realizations made me discover that *being cool* wasn't cool at all.

Coolness is perspectival. I discovered that things have no meaning. Or, rather, material items have only the meaning we give them. You can think buying a forty thousand dollar car is cool, or you can believe riding public transportation is cool. Neither is right or wrong—it's all based on your perspective. It's up to you to decide what is cool. You don't have to let TV, radio, magazines, or people on the Internet tell you what is cool.

Real friends don't give a shit about cool. Why was I so concerned with fancy things? Was it going to make people respect me more, like me more, love me more? No, of course not. Besides, anyone who respected me because of the car I drove didn't respect *me* anyway: they respected the idea of me, but not me—the me on the inside. Ryan will always be my friend, even if I wear a Jockey teeshirt and ride the bus to his house. He doesn't care about that stuff: he cares about me. He is a real friend, and I'm thankful to have a lot of great people like him in my life.

I met truly cool people. My friends are atypically cool (though they vehemently deny it). They are acute listeners; they are honest, genuine, trusting, trustworthy—all virtues I consider to be tremendously cool. My friends have taught me that being cool has nothing to do with the stuff I own and everything to do with the way I act, the way I treat other people, the way I contribute—those are the attributes that make people cool.

HEY, LOOK AT ME! I'M RELEVANT, DAMMIT!

Driving through the Midwest after weeks in the Mountain Time Zone creates an interesting juxtaposition. Navigating the terrifying interstates between Kansas City, Indianapolis, and Cincinnati, one can't help but notice the sprawl, the gridlock, the cacophony of road noise. Although some of the best people on earth reside in the heartland, there seems to be a sort of ever-present, east-of-the-Rockies angst there, too.

Walking the streets of downtown St. Louis, the overwhelming sounds were unavoidable: People blared car horns with anger. Passersby bellowed into mobile phones. Pedestrians argued loudly on street corners.

Everything seemed caffeinated.

If you step back and listen, though, it quickly becomes obvious what all the fuss is about: we make noise because we want to be heard, and because it's a loud world, we're forced to shout amid the backdrop of chaos.

Ultimately, we're screaming, tooting our anger-horns, and disrespecting other people in an effort to feel relevant. Too often, we treat the people we love like shit—not to make ourselves feel better, but to make us feel less bad—an ephemeral solution to a perpetual discontent.

Tearing down everyone else's buildings doesn't make our building any taller, though. Likewise, being the loudest or most angry noisemaker doesn't make us any more relevant.

Real relevance—true, lasting importance in this world—comes from the influence we yield, and influence comes from our ability to contribute beyond ourselves—to add value to other people's lives. We are considerably more relevant when we help the people around us build taller buildings.

Otherwise, we're just adding to the noise, which makes it hard to hear the soft, beautiful whisper of the world around us.

EVERYDAY MINIMALISTS

People often ask us whether there are any "normal" minimalists out there. Meaning: are there any minimalists who make a living in more conventional ways than, say, writing? Are there minimalist teachers, bankers, factory workers, engineers, architects, lawyers, security guards, plumbers, grocery-store clerks?

The short answer is: yes, thousands.

While on tour, we've met thousands of minimalists who lead comparatively conventional lives—from CEOs, salesmen, and professors, to philanthropists, social workers, and rabbis.

Why don't we ever hear their stories?

While this may seem like an irksome paradox, it's just common sense: the few minimalists who share their journeys are, by definition, more well-known than the ones who don't.

Take, for example, our friends Jamar, a teacher in Cincinnati; Adam, a pastor in Tennessee; and Jessica and Matt, an awesome couple in Los Angeles. Although they are minimalists, rarely do these people boast publicly over their simpler lives; rather, they use minimalism privately as a tool to focus less on consumption and more on health and relationships, experiences and creativity.

It is difficult to point to these people as examples of everyday minimalists, because simple living is part of their *interior* lives. They are private citizens, and for obvious reasons we rarely see public illustrations of their journeys. (By the way, this is why we interviewed dozens of them for our upcoming documentary—to shed light on the silent majority.)

There are many different flavors of minimalism. Minimalists who publicly share their journey—people such as Courtney Carver, Patrick Rhone, Allen Coltrane, et al.—present their recipes in hopes others may glean insight and spoon out a few ingredients to create their own flavor of minimalism, using their own recipe.

These sharers—bloggers, authors, and speakers—are just the tip of the iceberg. For every one minimalist who shares her journey with the masses, there are thousands who live their private lives with more meaning, but less stuff.

CHAPTER TEN || **Passion**

UNAMERICAN DREAM

THE AMERICAN DREAM

The white picket fence. The large suburban home. The luxury car. The big-screen TVs glowing in multiple rooms. The safe, reasonable nine-to-five. The corner office. The suit and tie. The white-collar pride. The blue-collar pride. The weekends off. The paid holidays. The occasional vacation. The fringe benefits.

IN EXCHANGE FOR

The daily grind. The nose to the grindstone. The rush-hour traffic. The punching the clock. The cubical farms. The spreadsheet eyestrain. The much-anticipated lunch break. The inbox overflow. The arbitrary goals. The late nights at the office. The empty platitudes. The office gossip. The "productivity." The downsizing. The "doing more with less." The mounds of bills. The second job. The credit-card spending. The debt. The second mortgage. The beer gut. The midlife crisis. The retirement at 65. The volatile stock market. The retirement at 67 or 72 or 75. The death before retirement. The unyielding tiredness. The emptiness. The depression. The unshakeable discontent.

You can keep your American Dream. Give us back our time, our freedom, and our lives.

UNTEACHERS

The more experienced we are, the more unlearning we must do.

We enter this world as creators, curious to discover ways to express ourselves visually, auditorily, kinesthetically. Over time, though, we are taught to be more "realistic," to be "safe" and "reasonable" and "normal." We never wanted to be safe or reasonable. Maybe we wanted to be normal, but today's normality template is far from what most of us had in mind at age five.

Growing up, we all just wanted to be ourselves: *that* was normal. Soon we were placed in a classroom, told to stand in line, speak when spoken to, and prescribed ADHD medication if we got out of line. This methodology worked great for creating factory workers and farmers, which seemed ideal when 90% of the population was either the former or the latter.

Today, however, most people are neither factory workers nor farmers (and even those positions have changed radically in the past few decades), and yet we're all graced with the assembly-line mentality, systematically programmed for compliance, expected to adhere to external standards while disregarding whatever our own internal normal was.

During this process, our creativity is quashed and replaced with a vast emptiness, a desire to create, even though we're told we're not creative. It's no coincidence we start focusing more on consuming around the same time, looking for any(material)thing to fill the void.

"All children are artists. The problem is how to remain an artist once he grows up." Picasso had this observation a century ago, and, unfortunately, these words ring even truer in today's postindustrial world, a world where our vocations no longer ape the form of creation (a la farming and factorying), and thus the gap between creation and consumption widens as we attempt to buy what no one can possibly sell: individual creativity.

The strange thing about this antiquated system is that most of its gatekeepers—government officials, school administrators, and teachers—aren't operating out of malice: their reaction is birthed from apathy, comfort, or both. Many teachers are just as disenchanted with the whole mess as we are, although they often feel like just another faceless cog in the wheel, powerless amongst the tyranny of bureaucracy.

Thankfully, there are alternatives. For children there is home schooling, unschooling, and wonderful programs like 826 Valencia. For adults the options are endless—there are books, blogs, classes, conferences. Plus there are scores of people like us (The Minimalists)—people who've rejected the system and aligned their lives with their values and beliefs—who function not as teachers, but as unteachers, helping people unlearn the bullshit they've acquired over the years, so they, too, can become unteachers and help further the spread of creativity and ideas.

None of these alternatives are easy, but then again it is way too easy to stand in line, to raise a hand when we want to speak, to blindly follow authority, to capitulate, and, above all, to *comply*. Screw that.

The easy route is easy because it's a vacuum, devoid of meaning, vacant. It also lacks innovation and beauty and all the unspeakable qualities that makes life exhilarating and worth living. The scenic route takes longer to travel, but the experience is worth it.

Also worth reading: Seth Godin's free manifesto, "Stop Stealing Dreams," at StopStealingDreams.com.

LIFE'S MOST DANGEROUS QUESTION
by Joshua Fields Millburn

What do you do? This is often the first question we ask strangers. On the surface it seems like an innocuous query, one we ask each other every day, a servile four-word nicety we utter so we have something—*anything*—to talk about.

The majority of the answers are boring, soundbite-ish replies we have standing by at the ready, prepped for the next dinner party or networking event: *I am a director of operations. I am a regional manager. I am the senior vice president of Who-Gives-A-Shit.*

Whoop-dee-do. Good for you.

Truth be told, we regurgitate these canned answers because they're easy to repeat, trance-like and semi-conscious, over and over and over again. No one wants to talk about their boring day job ad nauseam, but it sure is easy to state your name, rank, and serial number: it's easy to prove you're a cog in the wheel or a rung on the ladder —just like everyone else. It's much harder, however, to talk about other, more important aspects of life. So, instead of finding more worthwhile discussions, we go about our days providing lifeless answers to this lifeless question, our collective discs set to repeat.

Let's think about this question: it's such a broad, salient inquiry any answer would suffice. What do I do? I do a lot of things: I drink water. I eat food. I write words sloppily onto little yellow legal pads.

Once you scrape away its cheap gold-plating, however, you'll find a series of irksome inquisitions lurking beneath the surface. Sadly, what we're actually asking when we posit this malefic question, albeit unknowingly, is:

How do you earn a paycheck? How much money do you make? What is your socioeconomic status? And based on that status, where do I fall on the socioeconomic ladder compared to you? Am I a rung above you? Below you? How should I judge you? Are you worth my time?

There is a better way to answer this dangerous query, though: by changing the question altogether.

The next time someone asks what you do, try this: Don't give them your job title. Instead, tell them what you're passionate about, and then change course by asking them what they are passionate about:

"What do you do?" asks the stranger.

"I'm passionate about writing (or rock climbing or sailing or input accounting)," you say, followed by, "What are you passionate about?"

At this point, you'll likely get one of three responses: 1) a blank stare, 2) the person will tell you they're also passionate about X, Y, or Z, and the conversation will veer off in a more heartfelt direction, or 3) the stranger will attempt to recite their job title, to which you can respond, "That's great. So you're passionate about your job?" Eventually, you will both discuss the things you enjoy, instead of the jobs you don't.

I practiced this exercise during my last year in the corporate world: it helped me remove the importance of my job title from my life, and it opened me up to discussing with others my passion for writing. I had an impressive job title, but it didn't make me happy—it didn't fulfill me. Now I'm more fulfilled pursuing my dream than by any title.

Think of this shift as *changing a noun into a verb*. Instead of giving people a title (i.e., a box to put you in), let them know what you enjoy doing—what you're passionate about —and then discover what they enjoy. The conversation will morph into something far more interesting, and you'll learn a lot more about each other than your silly job titles.

WHAT IS YOUR MISSION?

You were not meant to do any *one* thing for the rest of your life.

Yet this idea of birthright passion is promulgated throughout our society, throughout the Internet in particular, as if each person has a preordained vocation he or she must pursue—as if evolution, natural selection, or whatever—has spent thousands of years plotting and transmogrifying so you can be a writer, a yoga teacher, or an astronaut.

Life doesn't contain these absolutes. No one has a predetermined destiny; no one has a singular preexisting passion waiting to be uncovered. There are dozens, even hundreds, of things you can do with your life—work you can be happy and passionate about. Hence, "follow your passion" is crappy advice.

What's important to consider, then, is this question: *What is my mission?*

Many of us go through life working a job or, worse, a career. We become accustomed to a particular lifestyle, a lifestyle that involves too much spending, personal debt, and consumer purchases—our own personalized version of the American Dream. Then we get stuck on the corporate ladder, and before we know it we're too high up to climb back down, so high up even looking down is a terrifying proposition. So we keep soldiering forward, onward and upward, without ever asking the important questions.

There's nothing inherently wrong with working a job: we all have to keep the lights on. However, when we travel too far from living a deliberate life—when we stop asking difficult questions—we stop feeling fulfilled.

Like your passion, your *mission* is not preexisting, and it's not always easy to find or pursue. When you find something—*anything*—you're passionate about and you make it your life's mission, you will find great joy and rewards in the work you do. Otherwise you're just earning a paycheck.

"FOLLOW YOUR PASSION" IS CRAPPY ADVICE
by Joshua Fields Millburn

Are you passionate about your life? Your job? Your hobbies? What are you passionate about? How do you incorporate those passions into your life?

These are important questions—questions closely linked to your happiness, contentment, and personal growth. I'm a big proponent of doing what you're passionate about, "following your passion"—so much so Ryan and I dedicated an entire chapter in our book *Minimalism: Live a Meaningful Life* to finding and pursuing your passions. Unfortunately, these days there are many passion-misers running around the Internet promulgating an irresponsible view of following your passion. While these people are often filled with good intentions, the end result of their advice—of dropping everything merely to follow your passion—can prove disastrous.

Ryan and I were fortunate enough to spend a few hours in a tiny classroom with our friend, Cal Newport, where we discussed life, habits, discipline, and why "follow your passion" is bullshit advice.

Cal Newport, Ph.D., a 30-year-old assistant professor of computer science at Georgetown University, is interested in why some people lead successful, enjoyable, purpose-driven lives while so many others do not. Being a self-proclaimed geek (but still one of the coolest guys I know), Cal is not satisfied with simplistic slogans like "Follow your passion!" Instead, he dives deeper, looking to decode underlying patterns of success in all their nuanced glory.

I've always respected Cal for his contrarian viewpoints. His popular website, *Study Hacks*, is one of only a handful of blogs to which I subscribe.

Over the last two years, Cal has helped me shift my perspective on several key areas of my life, including the oversimplification of mantras like "follow your passion." In celebration of his new book, *So Good They Can't Ignore You*, I asked Cal the following questions.

JFM: The advice often regurgitated throughout the Internet is simply, "You should follow your passion." Why does this sound so appealing? Why is this bad advice?

Cal: It's appealing because it's both simple and daring. It tells you that you have a calling, and if you can discover it and muster the courage to follow it, your working life will be fantastic. A big, bold move that changes everything: this is a powerful storyline.

The problem is that we don't have much evidence that this is how passion works. "Follow your passion" assumes: a) you have preexisting passion; and b) if you match this passion to your job then you'll enjoy that job.

When I studied the issue, it was more complex. Most people don't have preexisting passions. And research on workplace satisfaction tells that people like their jobs for more nuanced reason than simply it matches some innate interest.

JFM: You advocate *cultivating* your passion, instead of *following* your passion. What are the key differences?

Cal: "Follow" implies that you discover the passion in advance then go match it to a job. At which point, you're done.

"Cultivate" implies that you work toward building passion for your job. This is a longer process but it's way more likely to pay dividends. It requires you to approach your work like a craftsman. Honing your ability, and then leveraging your value, once good, to shape your working life toward the type of lifestyle that resonates with you.

JFM: In your research, what were some of the most common misconceptions you discovered about following your passion?

Cal: The biggest issue I run into is semantic. When I say, "don't follow your passion," some people get upset because they think I am saying, "don't follow the goal of being passionate about your work." But I'm not saying this. Passion is great. I just don't see a lot of evidence that passion is something that exists naturally waiting to be discovered. It takes hard work and planning to develop.

JFM: In a recent speech, you told people to, "Do as Steve Jobs did, not as he said." I thought this was great advice. Can you expand on it?

Cal: Steve Jobs, in his famous Stanford Commencement address, told the students (and I'm paraphrasing here): *You've got to find what you love, don't settle.*

If you read the press and social media that surrounded the event, it's clear that many people interpreted this as him saying, "follow your passion." If you go back into the details of his biography, however, you discover this is not what he did. He stumbled into Apple computer (it was a scheme to make a quick $1,000) at a time when he was "passionate" mainly about eastern mysticism.

But Jobs was open to opportunity. When he sensed that his scheme was bigger than he imagined, he pivoted and poured a lot of energy into building a company around selling computers. He cultivated passion. He didn't follow it.

JFM: Often times, people get excited about an idea, but they quickly lose steam and soon lose their drive to see their idea through. Why does this happen? How can we rectify this problem?

Cal: An issue here is that we rarely talk about what true passion feels like. The sensation of excitement about a particular idea is often a different sensation than the type of deep passion that drives people into a fulfilling career. Excitement comes and goes. True passion arises after you've put in the long hours to really become a craftsman in your field and can then leverage this value to really have an impact, to gain autonomy and respect, to control your occupational destiny.

JFM: If someone is lost and she doesn't know what her passion is, what first step do you recommend to get her on the right track toward cultivating her passion?

Cal: Here's the key: there is no special passion waiting for you to discover. Passion is something that is cultivated. It can be cultivated in many, many different fields. Therefore, it doesn't make sense to say, "I don't know what my passion is." What does make sense is to say, "I haven't yet cultivated a passion, I should really focus down on a small number of things and start this process."

TOO MUCH BRANDING THESE DAYS

by Joshua Fields Millburn

There is a difference between a *brand* and *branding*. McDonald's, Johnson & Johnson, and Walmart are brands. And *you*, if you're a creator of something, can also be a brand. The difference between a *corporation* as a brand and *you* the brand is the corporation's primary objective is, by definition, to make money. *You*, on the other hand, needn't bear profit as your main objective.

If *you the maker* are concerned principally with earning money by creating something, and yet you pretend this something is being made to benefit the greater good, then your product will reek of insincerity, pretense, and disingenuousness. This is commonplace for corporations, so much so we've come to expect it in their advertisements —we know their fundamental goal is money.

For example, have you ever believed a corporation truly understands *you*? I certainly haven't—not as an adult, at least. But I have regarded as true that certain musicians, authors, or artists understand *me* as a person—there is often a connection between me, the artist, and her work.

This doesn't mean products devised for profit aren't useful (they often are), it simply means people won't find the same connection with that product as they do with the literature, music, or artwork they love—for the main objective of these personal works isn't (typically) financial in nature, it is to develop a connection with other human beings.

When making money is the dominant driver for what you create, you are *branding*—carefully composing your image, neurotically considering your demographic, and obsessively tweaking your good or service to fit a customer base.

There's nothing wrong with earning money—I simply prefer for it to result from what I write (not the other way around). I've found when I'm honest, open, and add value to other people's lives, people are willing to support my work whenever they are given the opportunity.

THE PROBLEM WITH CORPORATIONS

by Joshua Fields Millburn

A lot of people think I'm anti-corporation. I am not.

I don't think corporations are innately bad or evil. Corporations—large ones in particular—*are* inherently problematic, though, because their primary objective is, by definition, to make money.

There's nothing wrong with bringing in revenue—I'm certainly not allergic to earning an income—but when it's the central focus, which it has to be for a large corporation, then the wrong lines tend to get real blurry real quick as the bosses' collective feet are held to the fire.

I've seen it too many times—an upstanding, respectable person ignoring his values, bending his ethics, and exhausting his moral gas tank just to aid the bottom line. (I know, because I did it myself in my corporate days of yesteryear: that's why I left.)

Bending one's principles in the name of profit or capitalism is not celebrating the true nature of capitalism at all.

A small business or individual, however, can earn money while their main focus is on something more rewarding—be it creating, innovating, growing, or cultivating a passion. So, yes, I'm wary of corporations—but I'm heartily supportive of the people who work for them to feed their families.

NOT HEREDITARY
by Joshua Fields Millburn

I have a confession: I am *not* a natural writer—I'm more of a natural basketball player than I am a writer.

Another confession: I didn't read my first book until I was 21. No, that's not a typo: I was 21 years old when I read my first book cover to cover, a pop-trash thriller. On the other hand, I was 6'2" in eighth grade, and thus basketball seemed pretty natural at the time.

As time marched on, and I stopped getting taller and my dribbling skills stopped improving, basketball became less and less natural. Years later, I discovered literary fiction at age 22, and I knew I wanted to take part in its creation: I knew I wanted to be a part of literature's exchange of consciousness. I knew I wanted to be a writer.

There was just one problem: my writing sucked. I didn't know anything—Not. A. Damn. Thing.—about mechanics, usage, grammar, or spelling. I could hardly cobble together a coherent independent clause, let alone a sentence that felt urgent, interesting, or vaguely alive. Although I wasn't gifted with a congenital writing quill, I soldiered on: I kept writing, letting most of the words hit the wastebasket shortly after they dribbled from my keyboard.

As I persisted in my studies and practice of the craft—guess what—I got better. And while practice didn't make perfect, it allowed me to grow considerably. Later, my growth snowballed, and now, a decade after reading my first book, I've published several bestsellers.

Writing was never natural for me. Most things in life aren't innate: individual betterment has little to do with inbred talent. I try to pound this fact into my writing students' noggins every chance I get: any teacher worth his chalk dust can teach techniques that will help you grow, but individual betterment requires practice and dedication and, to a certain extent, a healthy obsession.

And hence this essay is not about writing, and it's certainly not about me. This essay is about you, so take note: many people—people like you and me—want to do something different with their lives (I know I did), but most of these people think their would-be actions are futile because, well, because they weren't born with natural talent. These folks feel helpless or defeated, so they never take the first steps, and they certainly don't dedicate the hours required to develop real talent.

Life doesn't work this way: for any dimension of life, for any skill set—be it exercise, ballroom dancing, or guitar playing —you must be willing to drudge through the drudgery to find the joy on the other side. Before a man can even think about being a rockstar, he must earn the calluses on his fingertips.

To do this effectively, you must find ways to make the menial work more fun. After much practice—many, many hours of practice—whatever you're doing eventually feels like second nature, which is better in countless ways: second nature always feels more earned, more honest, more real.

CREATE YOUR MASTERPIECE
by Joshua Fields Millburn

Do you wish you could create something meaningful? Do you wish you had the time to work on that thing you've always wanted to produce—that novel, that piece of art, that passion project?

No need to keep wishing your life away. Based on my experience—years of procrastination, followed by a couple years of rigorous work, resulting in two personal masterpieces—I've written a 16-step guide to get you started on your own masterpiece.

If I could fire up the DeLorean and rewind the last decade, this is everything I would tell my 21-year-old self about creating purposeful work. It would have been harsh—but I needed it, and it would have saved me a ton of heartache. Feel free to listen in.

Step 1. Look yourself in the mirror. It's time for you to be honest with yourself, young Josh. Either you're accomplishing what you want to accomplish or you're not—there is no in-between. If it's the latter, then you must admit to yourself *you* are the only person preventing you from pursuing your passion project. Denial is a heartless bitch, so the first step is looking in the mirror and admitting you haven't even scratched the surface on creating something significant.

Step 2. Kill your distractions. Make a list of everything getting in your way. Surfing the Internet too much? Get rid of the Internet at home. Certain people draining all your time? Get rid of your shitty relationships. Material possessions getting in the way? Get rid of your crap.

Step 3. Make time every day. None of us were born equal. We come from different backgrounds, different cultures, different socioeconomic situations. We are not all born on a level playing field—time is our only equalizer. We all have the same 24 hours in a day. So, get up at 3:30 a.m. if you must. Find 30 minutes before you leave for work. Work through your lunch break. Find an hour after work. If you want it bad enough, you'll find the time. You have the same amount of time as everyone else who has ever created a masterpiece.

Step 4. Stop making excuses. *I should do this. I should do that. I should, I should, I should.* Too often, we should all over ourselves. You must instead make change a *must. I must create a masterpiece! I must make time every day! I must kill my distractions!* Those *musts* sound far more empowering than your *shoulds*, don't they?

Step 5. Stop worrying. Most people are going to praise you for what you do—they'll be proud of your masterpiece once it's finished. But instead we tend to worry about the naysayers. Guess what: people are going to judge you. Some people are going to think what you're doing is stupid. Others will think you've lost your mind. What other people think doesn't matter: they will be dead soon, and so will you and I. Better get to work.

Step 6. Grow a pair of balls.

Step 7. Take incremental action. Nearly all masterpieces share two commonalities: time and action. You must do the work every day. You won't create your masterpiece overnight, so don't try: it's far more important to work on it each day. In the course of time, your daily actions will add up immensely. Eventually, you'll look in life's rearview mirror and everything will be different.

Step 8. Change your physiology. Your brain and your body aren't standing in opposite corners of the room: if you want to stimulate your mind, you must stimulate your body. Do something physical: Walk. Run. Hit the gym. Try yoga. Breathe. Exercise for eighteen minutes a day. Trek 500 miles. Just do something to get your body moving: motion creates emotion.

Step 9. Focus. Focus on your masterpiece. Whatever you focus on, you'll create. Think your project is crappy? Then it will be crappy. Think you'll get it done no matter the odds? Then you'll finish it even if you get hit by a bus.

Step 10. Change your beliefs. One of the biggest reasons we don't accomplish what we set out to accomplish is our limiting beliefs. For years you've told yourself you'll never be this, you'll never be that, you'll never be good enough —but you're no different from the people who have constructed their masterpieces. The people who create something special—something lasting—aren't necessarily smarter, funnier, better, or more toothsome than you: they simply believed they could do it, and through this belief they didn't let anything stand in their way.

Step 11. Become obsessed. Half of passion is love—the other half, obsession. Your masterpiece will feed off your obsession, growing mightily the more obsessed you become. Eventually, you'll wake up thinking about it. You'll go to bed thinking about it. You'll think about it in the bathroom stall. This is good. Let your masterpiece become your obsession. Let it take over.

Step 12. Cut the fat. Brevity is the soul of wit. Or perhaps, more accurately, brevity is wit. Julien Smith's book, *The Flinch*, is intentionally brief. The entire thing can be tweeted, page by page, line by line. Every line was carefully considered. Same goes for *Everything That Remains*—years of work, boiled down to a couple hundred pages. Sure, a masterpiece can be longer and more oblique and digressive—but does it need to be? Realize you, too, can build something massive and then chisel it down to its essence. Do this and people will find value in your work.

Step 13. Get the old guard out of the way. Are gatekeepers getting in your way? Can't talk to the person you want to pitch? Can't find an agent or a publisher willing to give you the time of day? Can't get on CNN or MTV? So what! Do it yourself. For the first time in history, you don't need the old guard. We live in an era where the Indians can circumvent the chiefs, taking their masterpieces straight to the tribe. (Learn about our indie-publishing recipe at Asymmetrical.co/how-to.)

Step 14. Make it inexpensive. Money was never the goal of your masterpiece, was it? No, you wanted people to hear your album, read your book, or view your art—to see, hear, feel, smell, and taste your masterpiece. So remove your boundaries and make it inexpensive. Let it go. It's no longer yours anyway—it belongs to the world.

Step 15. Breathe. Pause and bask in the glory of your masterpiece. Go ahead—take it all in. Enjoy the moment, you deserve it.

Step 16. Do it again. Return to step one and get started on your next masterpiece. This lifetime can contain as many masterpieces as you create.

THE DETAILS
by Joshua Fields Millburn

Daily life is overwhelming: each day we are faced with an unforgiving barrage of in-your-face advertisements, with "calls to action," and with half-a-million bits of unsolicited data. Amongst this information avalanche, it's difficult to discern which details are relevant and which are not.

It is, however, the details that make life interesting, exciting, and, most of all, memorable. The details are important; both God and the devil reside there. Without life's myriad particulars, our lives lack variety—and without variety, we quickly get bored out of our skulls.

To illustrate:

Last year's Misfit Con was, without doubt, the best conference I've attended (and I've attended scores). It wasn't special because of an expensive light show, some brand new technology, or even because I spoke there—it was special because of its intentionality and the overwhelming attention paid to the small things.

AJ and Melissa Leon, Misfit's founders, focused fervently on the details: they didn't hold the event in your typical conference-type location, like New York or California, opting instead for Fargo, North Dakota, a city surprisingly erumpent with creativity. AJ and Melissa involved the local community, too, intertwining neighborhood artists, musicians, and writers into the proceedings. And they didn't attempt to "scale-up" the affair, opting instead for handcrafted everything, from the surprise venues and full-time onsite barista, to the custom artwork on the walls and bright flowers hanging overhead like vibrant stalactites. They even curated not just the event's guest speakers, but also the audience, deciding to limit the number of attendees to fewer than 150, requiring an approved application to attend (hundreds of people from all over the world applied, only a fraction were accepted). The whole thing was, in a word, unforgettable.

In fact, every memory we hold—good or bad—is comprised of absorptive details. We remember outstanding conferences like Misfit because people like AJ and Melissa are obsessed with getting the details right: the handcraftedness, the personal touch, the careful curation. Conversely, we remember a restaurant's terrible service because of the little things they got wrong: the overcooked meat, the apathetic waiter, the crumbs on the table.

Without the details, though, the experience is neither good nor bad: it is transactional. No one ever remembers the transaction—transactions are banal by nature.

Get bogged down with too many details, and life quickly becomes overwhelming, unbearable—vanquished with sensory overload. It is our job to distinguish the 2% of the details that are important from the unimportant 98%.

This is a lesson I teach in my online writing class: a great story highlights the essential 2% by *eliminating* the superfluous 98%. Only then does the story become interesting, only then is the reader absorbed into something more meaningful. This was true for the Misfit Con: it was remarkable not only because of the attention to detail, but because of the deliberate attention to *meaningful* details.

The same holds true for any well-curated life: of those half a million daily inputs, the key is to highlight the few dozen that are actually important—the details that add value to our lives. Often, the best way to do so is to start eliminating —to get rid of the excess that makes life opaque so that everything worthwhile shines through.

The details are direly important—being obsessed with the *right* details is even more important.

COLA AND POLITICS

"There is no such thing as not voting: you either vote by voting, or you vote by staying home and tacitly doubling the value of some Diehard's vote."
—David Foster Wallace

Another big election is peeking its gigantic, mass-mediated noggin around the corner. It's almost here, and if we rely solely on the U.S. media for our info, then we might believe we have only two choices: Democrat vs. Republican.

Believing there are only two voting options is like assuming we have only two beverage choices: Coke vs. Pepsi. Sure, you might enjoy the taste of one over the other, but they're both essentially the same thing. That choice is a faux-choice, and thus not much of a choice at all.

The truth is we have myriad options, not just Coke or Pepsi, not just Democrat or Republican. We can choose to live more consciously, realizing and understanding our options. Instead of cola, we can drink water or green drinks; instead of the main political parties, we can vote Libertarian or Green Party (or write in Ryan Nicodemus). Irrespective of our choice, we can ignore what we're "supposed" to do and, instead, follow our hearts.

Some people might argue you're throwing away your vote, but if you follow your heart, it's never in vain—even when you know you're going to lose. That goes for relationships, health, politics, or any other area of life—if you follow your heart, you can lose only once; but if you don't, you may lose a thousand times, a trail of scattered regrets strewn throughout the landscape in the rearview.

We have no interest in propagating our own political views here; rather, we simply want to encourage you to be true to yourself. Drink your pop and vote the party line if that's what your heart tells you to do; if it doesn't, there are always other options.

COURSE CORRECTION

Pencils have erasers for a reason: everyone makes mistakes; everyone makes bad decisions.

To err is human; therefore, one of the most important skills we can develop is *course correction*. It's direly important to understand when a mistake is a mistake, to learn from our indiscretions, and then to change course and move forward a better person.

Life is a test, and sometimes we pick the wrong answer. No big deal, right? Unfortunately we often pick the same wrong answer over and over, avoiding any other possible outcome, and therefore avoiding the correct answer. It's strange, we wouldn't've done this with our old schoolroom tests. We never filled in the answer bubble on our Scantron sheet just to erase it and fill in the same bubble again and again and again.

In real life we do this all the time: we mess up and then take the same path, which leads to the same failure. And then we do it again. And again. And again.

To make things more complicated, life's answers change as we get older; therefore, yesterday's right answer may not be today's right answer.

To live an enriched, fulfilled life, one must hone his ability to course correct. If you can intelligently assess where you are, where you're headed, and make the necessary tweaks to move forward, then you'll be just fine; but if you keep filling in the same bubble, you're in for a world of bad marks.

CHAPTER ELEVEN || **Contribution**

ADDING VALUE

Contributing to someone's life is one of the most important things you can do: it is the only way to get another person's unmitigated buy-in and is one of the few ways to get other people to believe in you. Obviously, this is important in all facets of life—in leadership positions, in friendships, while meeting and connecting with new people, at your job, with your family.

If you want people to respect you, then you must add value to their lives. There are many ways one can add value:

Create something someone can use.
Inspire someone to take action.
Lend a helping hand.
Be a shoulder to cry on.
Show someone how to do something.
Show someone a better way.
Provide a new perspective.
Lead by example.

Listen more.
Give your full attention.
Just be there for someone.
Love them.

It's important to contribute in an authentic way, one without an ulterior motive—genuine, helpful, and unassuming.

We have all benefited from someone's giving nature. The two of us started our website because we were inspired and encouraged by the value created by several people. Those people added value to our lives, enough value that we were compelled to change and improve our lives; thus, we find it important to add value to other people whenever we can—to pay it forward.

Who adds value to your life? How do you add value to others?

ASK NOT WHAT YOU CAN GET

Last night in Atlanta, amid the overwhelming tall buildings and sexy Southern accents, someone asked us a question: *Why are you doing this?* The implicit question was: *What do you plan on getting from dedicating a year of your lives to a 100-city free tour?*

It's strange: we don't look at it this way. We're not on the road for ten months to *get* anything—ours is a journey of giving.

We do, however, get satisfaction from adding value to

others' lives—but that's not all we *get*. We always get more whenever we *give*.

It's cringeworthy whenever we see people who attempt to get without first giving, to take without contributing. Scientists have a name for this kind of organism: a parasite.

The key to giving, then, is simple: add value *first* without any expectation of receiving anything in return. Do this with enough frequency and you'll get way more than you give.

As a result of our giving, people have given back to us immensely: *Everything That Remains* reached the top ten of *all* books on Amazon as of the date of this writing (thank you!). More than 75,000 people RSVP'd for our last tour. We've been featured all over the media, and more than 4 million people will read our words this year. It turns out when you add value to other people's lives, they're eager to share the message with their friends and family— to add value to their lives. Adding value is a basic human instinct.

That's why we do this: we hope to serve others. Everything else is a wonderful bonus.

HERE, HAVE AN ORGAN
by Joshua Fields Millburn

There's usually a serpentine line snaked out the door at the Department of Motor Vehicles—at least that's always been my experience. Burnt into my memory are half-a-lifetime of Kafkaesque memories, nightmarish recollections of time spent waiting for assistance among the zombies and cobwebs at the DMV.

Surprisingly, when I visited the DMV recently in Missoula, Montana, there was no line at all. It was a different world: I was helped right away. I didn't even have to take one of those flimsy paper numbers from the dispenser by the entrance; and to boot, the Missoula DMV employees were fast, fastidious, and friendly.

I sat down and filled out the necessary forms to obtain a new driver's license. These forms seemed attenuated and easier to grasp than the bureaucratic stack I used to wrestle with back in Dayton, Ohio. It was too easy: name, address, DOB, etc., etc. And then my pen stopped as it hovered over the final question:

Do you want to be an organ donor?

I paused at this simple question. I'd never considered becoming an organ donor—not for lack of caring, but because of sheer ignorance of the statistics. Toward the end of last year, though, my friend Amanda emailed me a similar question: *How familiar are you with the organ transplant waiting list?*

Not at all, I responded.

She informed me there're 117,000 people in the U.S. alone who are waiting for organ transplants right now: 74,000 of them are active, which means that 74,000 people are in critical condition and unable to work, to play with their kids, to eat normally, to walk up a flight of stairs, to pick up a carton of milk at the grocery—you name it. Only about

20,000 of these people will actually receive a transplant in the next year, and it's not uncommon for a candidate to spend months in a hospital bed waiting for help. So consider this: one organ donor can save up to eighteen lives, and all he or she has to do is check a box on a driver's license application.

For the first time in my life, I checked the "yes" box on the form, and thus I'm now an organ donor. Perhaps you'll consider becoming one, too.

Ryan and I often write about the value of uncovering happiness in life. A large part of that happiness involves contribution. Giving is living, but I'm also comforted to know even when I die, I will still be able to contribute to others. After I take my last breath, my body will be dead, but because of my choice—my decision to check that affirmative box at the DMV—someone else will live.

Find more facts at the United Network for Organ Sharing (www.unos.org).

REPAYING INTELLECTUAL DEBT

How does one repay an intellectual debt?

We received this question in a kind, handwritten letter from a reader named Suravi. She wanted to know how to pay back the value we've added to her life. She wondered how she could repay us for sharing our thoughts, for sharing our journey, for helping her see the option she'd been given wasn't the only option in life.

Our answer: don't pay it back, pay it forward.

There are many people who have helped the two of us become the men we are today—people whose words and ideas have shaped who we are, people whom we'll never be able to compensate for the value they've provided: the type of value that isn't labeled with a price tag.

So instead of requiting those people, we choose to pay it forward. We go to great lengths to share our story, to document our myriad changes, so people can discover alternative paths toward happiness. With the exception of our books, the vast majority of what we write is free, which is our small way to contribute to the world.

You see, some debts you can repay only by traversing the world with kindness, respect, and intentionality. Such truisms might sound trite or cliche, but they become self-evident once you consider the value already bestowed upon you and you begin to pay it forward.

CHAPTER TWELVE || **Success**

THE SUCCESS TEMPLATE

by Joshua Fields Millburn

Success is not always self-evident—or rather, failure sometimes wields the shiny facade of success.

A recent *Inc.* magazine cover story featured the "Entrepreneur of the Year," Aaron Levie, a steel-eyed, suit-and-tie-clad, 28-year-old startup founder with an impressive track record. The handsome CEO brandishes all the accoutrements of a respect-worthy businessman: he is well spoken, he has a firm grasp on innovation and business strategy, he is funny and smart and charismatic, and, above all, he displays a steadfast work ethic. When unchecked, though, it's this latter virtue that can be problematic.

Inside its pages, the organ chronicled the young centimillionaire's stringent daily routine: "He wakes at around 10. He showers quickly and arrives at the office by 11 a.m. He downs two coffees, sometimes holding two cups at once. He rarely eats breakfast or, for that matter, lunch. He spends 90 percent of his daylight hours in meetings or interviews, to which he walks very quickly or even runs. … [At 8:30 p.m., after a one-hour nap, Levie] gets really, really productive. Each night, he sends a couple hundred emails [until] 2 or 3 a.m. … [He] does not take weekends off, and, in the last handful of years, he has taken [only] one vacation, a three-day trip to Mexico with his girlfriend."

I was impressed when I first read the above account—it's hard not to be, since we tend to base success on the post–Industrial Revolution standards we've established. After reading it again, though, I quickly shifted from impressed to depressed.

You see, Levie's daily program seemed much like my corporate routine of yesteryear—on steroids. It was a regimen that nearly killed me (and has turned Levie's hair prematurely gray), but the venture capitalists interviewed by the magazine applauded this relentless schedule, endorsing Levie's nonstop pace as the new paragon of success.

If that's what success looks like, then color me unsuccessful —I want no part of it.

Please don't mistake my words, though: I'm not condemning Aaron Levie. I'm not even objecting to his Energizer Bunny–esque days. With a nine-figure net worth, it's obvious he isn't doing it for the money—like I was, blindly.

Instead, I denounce the ideology that says working every waking hour is the template of success—it's not. Success is perspectival: it doesn't have a template. Aaron Levie is successful because he's doing what he wants to do with his life, and he's contributing to the lives of others (his company employees nearly 1,000 people). However, a stay-at-home dad can be just as successful.

Success is a simple equation: *Happiness + Constant Improvement + Contribution = Success.*

What's important, then, is to construct a life that aligns with your values and beliefs, your interests and desires. A life that makes you happy and adds value to others. If it doesn't, the shiny facade will eventually rust from the inside.

LIFE IS AN ACQUIRED TASTE
by Joshua Fields Millburn

The best coffeehouse in the United States isn't located in Seattle, Portland, New York City, or any of the usual suspects: Press Coffee Bar is nestled between a parking lot and a sewing shop, across the street from a pair of abandoned warehouses and beneath several stories of old brick apartments in Dayton, Ohio—the birthplace of aviation, the cash register, and hundred-spoke gold rims.

I was sitting in Press recently, tucked in the back, enjoying a black coffee, a subtle milieu of roasted beans and Radiohead's *OK Computer* in the atmosphere around me. Back in Dayton for a spell, I was spending a lot of time there dotting the I's and crossing the T's in our most recent book, *Everything That Remains*.

The shop's tattooed proprietors, Brett and Janell Barker, were, as usual, hard at work behind the counter. The Barkers are a husband-and-wife duo and are wonderful in more ways than one: friendly, attentive, passionate, and sticklers for detail. From the wood floors and wood-paneled walls, to the music and changed-monthly local-art installations, everything at Press is carefully and intentionally curated. Not to mention a handful of employees—Caleb, Awni, Brenden, Eric—who feel much more like family than staff, and customers who seem to embody a Cheers-esque camaraderie.

Then there's the coffee, of course: sourced from only the best roasters and brewed or pulled so carefully—so meticulously—it resembles art much more than foodservice. All of which culminates in the perfect coffeehouse: elegant, unpretentious, simple.

The simplicity of Press transcends the shop itself: not simple for the sake of being simple, Press is simple because they've eliminated the excess in favor of the essential. It was Brett, after all, who convinced me to do the same with my coffee.

I used to load my cup of joe with heaps of cream and sweetener until it was more a weak, milky, calorie-laden dessert than a drink. As I stirred in the excess, Brett would quietly rib me, encouraging me to enjoy the flavor without the additives.

I didn't listen. Not at first, at least—not until the day when they ran out of my sweetener of choice, and I was forced to go without. It was an unpleasant shock at first—drinking only coffee and cream—but soon my taste buds adjusted. I could better taste the coffee, and I went without sweetener from then on.

A month later, being the experimenter I am, I wondered what my coffee would taste like without milk, so I ordered an Americano and shook my head when Janell asked whether I wanted room for cream. Being unacclimated, the first sip was bitter—a strong punch to the palate. A few days in I acquired the taste, and for the first time in my life I could taste the actual coffee. It was more delicious than any of the sugary, weak, milky cups of yesteryear, and I never went back.

Black coffee is a synecdoche for life: when you eliminate the excess—when you deliberately avoid life's empty calories—what remains is exponentially more delicious, more enjoyable, more worthwhile. It might be a bitter shock at first; but, much like coffee, a meaningful life is an acquired taste. Sip slowly and enjoy.

THE RIGHT KIND OF FAME
by Joshua Fields Millburn

I'm back in North Dakota for a few days for a conference, and I can't help but laugh about the last time I was here.

Pretend your screen gets fuzzy as we flash back to this time last year:

I'm sitting with eight new friends in a sushi restaurant in downtown Fargo. I'm in town to speak at a conference. The restaurant's decor—drab walls, dim light, and wholesale furniture—is unremarkable. The staff here is adequate, not exactly friendly, not exactly not. The food is exquisite, though.

I'm working my way through a salmon roll while my new friends from the conference make light conversation, joking and laughing about this and that. Not one for small talk, I'm mostly listening—and masticating.

A lifelong novice with chopsticks, I force another piece of sushi into my mouth as I feel a tap on my shoulder. A petite blond girl is standing behind me, a look of trepidation on her pretty features. She appears either excited or nervous— or both. Perhaps a decade younger than me, she's too stylish to be employed by this establishment: dark denim, a white jacket, an asymmetrical haircut.

I attempt to say "hello," but with an awkward mouth full of rice I sound like a drowning man. My friend Colin, seated to my right, picks up my slack: "Sorry, but he's always this inarticulate around women."

I finally choke down the half-chewed salmon and garble a tentative greeting: "Hi."

"Hi," she responds with a bashful smile. "I'm sorry to bother you, but are you, umm … are you the guy on the cover of this book?" She's clutching a copy of *Minimalism: Live a Meaningful Life*, holding it with both hands, presenting it like a doctor would a newborn to its mother. A few people at the table snicker.

"Uhh … yes. That's me," I say, inspecting the cover as if verifying its authenticity.

"Wow! This is so cool. Would you sign it for me? And can I get a picture with you? Oh, this is so awesome! I can't believe it! I was just sitting over there reading your book, and now you're here. In this restaurant. In Fargo," she says.

I look over at Colin suspiciously, assuming he's the responsible party. I do get recognized from time to time, but come on: In a hole-in-the-wall sushi joint in North Dakota? In front of a bunch of impressive people who are clearly impressed by what's transpiring? By a pretty girl who just so happens to be reading my book at the same time I'm in town for a conference?

"Really?" I say, staring at Colin with incredulity.

"What?" he asks, an innocent look on his face.

"You set this up."

"Set *what* up?"

"This. You asked this girl to walk over here with my book."

"No, I didn't."

"Come on, man—no one's really going to believe this: the timing is too perfect. You're making us look ridiculous."

By now the rest of the table is listening, and the girl is still standing behind me, book in hand.

"I have no idea what you're talking about," Colin insists. He's a terrible liar, so, by his shocked expression, I can see he's telling the truth—he didn't set this up. This girl was not planted: none of this is rigged.

Hmmm…this must be what it feels like to be … ugh … "famous."

Oh, dear.

I take the napkin off my lap and stand. "Hi, I'm Joshua."

"I know," she laughs and extends a hand. "I'm Katie."

"I'm a hugger, Katie," I say and open both arms.

She gives me a big hug.

"Thanks for making me look much more impressive than I actually am, Katie."

She displays a white-toothed grin. "I'm only about halfway through the book, but it has already put things into a new perspective for me. It's like I'm asking myself all these new questions—questions I never even thought about asking before. You know, like about my material possessions, and about what I'm passionate about, and questions about my relationships. It's like this whole new way of looking at things."

That's when it clicked for me: It's not me who's famous. I am not what's interesting to people; rather, it's the message that's compelling, and I'm just the messenger—and I'm fine with that.

Actually, I imagine it'd be miserable to be truly famous—to

be famous for the sake of being famous, like Paris Hilton, the Kardashians, the entire cast of *Jersey Shore*. Those people are well-known only because they are famous—not for what they stand for, not for adding value to people's lives. (I'm not saying they're bad people, I just wouldn't want to be in their situations.)

When I'm recognized in public, however, it's usually accompanied by: "Aren't you one of The Minimalists?" or "Didn't you write that *Minimalism* book?" or "Thank you for your blog." I honestly never imagined I'd be a public figure, but now that I am eminent to a (very) small degree, I'm happy that what I'm known for is the right thing. Each time I'm recognized, I'm reminded our message is spreading—a message I sincerely believe in.

We all have an identity, but what we often don't realize is our identities are shaped by our daily actions. My daily actions of the last several years have made me a messenger for simple living: a designation I wear with pride.

Standing next to Katie as we pose for a photo together, I notice I'm a foot taller than her, which seems apropos since she isn't taking a picture with *me* anyway: she wants a photo next to minimalism, a movement taller than us all.

IF, THEN

People concoct all kinds of excuses to explain their bad decisions:

If I had more money, I could be happy.
If I had better genes, I could lose weight.
If I had more time, I could exercise more.
If I liked vegetables, I could eat healthier.
If I had gone to college, I could be successful.

If this, then that. It's the *if statement* that fails. Such utterances are debilitating self-fulfilling prophecies. They hold you back. The best thing to do is remove the *if* clause from your declarations, revealing your true potential:

I could be happy.
I could lose weight.
I could exercise more.
I could eat healthier.
I could be successful.

Because *if* you wanted to, you could live a meaningful life.

WHO TO EMULATE?

by Joshua Fields Millburn

A lifetime ago, when I was nineteen and starting to work my way up the corporate ladder, my boss gave me some valuable advice as I was reaching for the next rung far overhead: "Don't ask a man who earns $20,000 a year how to make $100,000."

I agreed at the time—and still agree now—but I have better advice: Don't ask an unhappy man how to become happy.

Too often we emulate someone without realizing we don't actually want to be like them. We look up to the person with the high-paying job, the prestigious career, or the material possessions for which we yearn, and we believe we want what they have—all the while not realizing how unhappy many of those people actually are.

Instead of emulating someone because of their accomplishments, then, it seems more prudent to emulate them for who they are: to learn from the person, not their facade of so-called achievements. There's nothing wrong with earning a shedload of money—it's just that the money doesn't matter if you're not happy with who you've become in the process.

A MINIMALIST, A JAPANESE COWBOY, AND AN ARROGANT AMERICAN WALK INTO A BAR
by Joshua Fields Millburn

I'm standing outside one my favorite places on earth, the Getty, next to an Asian man outfitted in rancher's attire: white cowboy hat, yellow snakeskin boots, head-to-toe denim. The views here are stunning: even under a ceiling of cerebral clouds, you can see miles in every direction. As I admire my surroundings, I think I finally understand the true meaning of the word "panoramic." With a galaxy of green hills to the south, downtown L.A.'s diffused skyline to the east, and a string of ruby taillights scorching the congested 405 to the north, the sun is preparing its decent into the hills of Santa Monica to our west, casting long, angular shadows before it disappears behind the Pacific's metallic horizon, like a glowing coin dropped carefully into a wishing well.

"I like your hat," I say to the denim-clad man, towering over him even with his heeled snakeskins.

"I like it, too," he responds definitively, with a thick Japanese accent and a nicotine smile, his cadence dressed in conviction. "I love living life," he says with no further explanation, as if everything that needed to be explained—about him, about life in general—is contained inside those four words. Although we've never met, the two of us are bystanders in the museum's afternoon architecture tour, which is just wrapping up. Our tour guide points out the 80,000-year-old granite pillars framing the impending sunset.

Behind us, an American man is complaining to his wife about the cold breeze, about the clouds overhead, about the lack of amplification in the tour guide's voice. He has been pompously protesting the entire tour. Apparently the universe has conspired to ruin his day. From the sound of his steadfast objections, everything here is ill-suited for his presence.

There should be something out of place with a five-foot-tall Japanese cattleman standing among Rembrandt paintings and modern architecture in Southern California, but there's not. Yet something is off with the everyday American grousing about the world's inadequacies.

Tuning out the American for a moment, I let the cowboy know he would fit in well back home in Montana. We have a lot of big hats and pickup trucks, I tell him. He says he likes that part of the country—"the Wild Western" he calls it—and then recommends a book called *The Solace of Open Spaces* by Gretel Ehrlich. (Although the book is out of print, I later found a copy online and discovered for myself Ehrlich's gorgeous rumination on life on Wyoming's high plains.)

Despite the cowboy's unconventional appearance, or maybe because of it, it is obvious he would fit in almost anywhere. His posture, his gait—even his gap-toothed grin —speak volumes about this man's interior life. He seems composed, resolute, content—miles from arrogant. He is: *confident.*

Conversely, no place seems fit for the babbling American. His regal standards and his poor expectations make assimilation a persistent problem. After another snarky comment directed toward his wife, I give him a searing eyeful, and his gaze immediately finds his feet. His bray may be the loudest here, but volume isn't a measure of confidence. A truly confident man need only whisper to be heard.

The sun is completing its coin toss into the ocean, our group outlined in twilight. Looking over the cowboy, surveying his staunch temperament, I realize his confidence is simply an external display of a rich interior life: congruency between his internal and external worlds. Arrogance, on the other hand, is the opposite of confidence: a veneer of composure, incongruence at its nadir. This is why a confident man is able to coalesce with any group, anywhere; an arrogant man, nowhere at all.

Confidence holds up under scrutiny, whereas arrogance

fractures with the slightest crack. And, as human beings, we all have cracks. Sooner or later, a spotlight is shone and the arrogant man's pomposity is exposed, seeping through the veneer, while the confident man just admires the beauty of his flaws.

THERE WILL BE BRUISES

We are driving through Mississippi. The air is crisper than we expected, an abrupt cold spell in the American South. After wonderful events in Tampa, Miami, Orlando, and Jacksonville, the Sunshine State has now receded into our rearview, but a bag of Florida-grown oranges still sits perched in the back seat.

Every so often, one of us reaches into the bag and removes a plump orange from the hoard. So juicy, so delicious. Occasionally, though, the citrus fruit we extract is less than ideal: underripe, slightly bruised, or even green and fuzzy with mold. *Bluck!* Like Gump's box of chocolates, you never know what you're gonna get.

You can, however, mitigate your risk. Like anything in life, you're going to get at least a few bad oranges. This is true even when you scrutinize the bag: there'll never be a perfect assemblage. So, whether we're buying oranges or a new home, we have three choices:

We can close our eyes, select any bag, and hope for the best.

We can hold out until we find the perfect selection.

We can choose carefully: pay attention, closely examine our options, and then pick the best.

The first option relies on luck (and laziness) to guide the way: don't be surprised if you end up with a bag of mold. The second option leads to discontent and starvation: there will never be a perfect bag. The third option is the intentional option: it optimizes the good, while understanding that no matter how hard you try, there will be bruises.

Intentionality requires more work, more deliberate action, but that's where all the reward is—an intentional life always tastes best.

WORTHY
by Ryan Nicodemus

I often feel unworthy. I face this feeling when I write about serious topics. I question whether I'm qualified to write about certain subjects, conjuring a tornado of negative thoughts: I'm not perfect. I'm not a Zen master. I'm not Dr. Nicodemus. I'm not worthy.

I could blame my upbringing for my psychological defect: I wasn't encouraged to be more than I was; however, I clearly remember being told what I wasn't. Whenever I catch myself inside this whirlwind of negative thought, I recognize what I'm doing and redirect my self-talk toward a more positive direction. Instead of what *I'm not*, I focus on what I *am*:

I am kind.

I am genuine.
I am adding value.
I am worthy.

Our level of self-worth is directly affected by the rules we've built for ourselves. If you have a rule for yourself that says, "I am not a baker if I don't own a bakery," then guess what: you're not going to feel worthy enough to call yourself a baker until you open a bakery.

Most of our internal rules have been shaped by years of reinforcement. That doesn't mean we must live by those rules for the rest of our lives, though. When we catch ourselves feeling unworthy, we should look for the rule we've established that makes us feel this way.

Regardless of what we've done in our pasts, we still get to decide our own levels of self-worth based on the rules we've established. As long as you are living up to those rules, you are worthy.

ELEMENTARY SCHOOL AND GRAD SCHOOL

There are many ways to learn. Many methods and techniques, many ways to acquire new skills, many teachers and mentors from whom we can gain knowledge.

One way is often referred to as "continuing education": graduate schools, trade schools, and various seminars and workshops offer this kind of study. This approach allows one to append his or her existing education, to build atop a firm foundation (or a shoddy one).

Another way is to start anew. Not unlike kindergarten, this manner of learning is simultaneously terrifying and exciting, because everything in the atmosphere is so new, so vivid, so uncertain and uncharted. Growth happens rapidly amid the terror and excitement of elementary school. (By the way, both emotions—terror and excitement—tend to conjure the same physiological reactions: rapid heartbeat, dilated pupils, sweaty palms. This type of attentiveness significantly aids personal growth.)

Both learning structures possess their advantages and disadvantages. Thankfully, in today's world, adults can have a hand in both methods, enjoying the fruits of uncharted territory while building upon the necessary bedrocks of an adult life.

For us, our move to Missoula, Montana, was both elementary school *and* grad school. We're still building on top of a sound structure, a solid foundation (*The Minimalists*), but we're also embracing the uncertainty of a new place with new people, a new business (Asymmetrical Press), and new daily practices and routines that will shape our growth in remarkable ways.

Elementary school can be terrifying, but you grow *through* the fear. Ultimately, you've won when your dreams have broken through your fears.

Eventually, we'll graduate kindergarten. What's new and exciting today will soon become routine, just another part of everyday life. When this happens, we'll need to move on to the next elementary-school experience if we want to keep growing—which we will. Without growth, people atrophy: we waste away, we die inside. To avoid this fate, we must continue to find new ways to grow, new elementary schools to crash.

How about you? What is your elementary school? How will it change over time?

30 LIFE LESSONS FROM 30 YEARS

by Joshua Fields Millburn

I recently turned 30, and during the journey I've learned a great deal. Following are 30 of the most important life lessons from my first 30 years on this planet.

1. **We must love**. You know the saying, "It's better to have loved and lost than never to have loved at all," right? I know, we often dismiss cliches with a wave of the hand, but maybe it's a truth so profound we can discuss it only with aphorisms. Yes, we must love, even if it breaks our hearts—because, unless we love, our lives will flash by.

2. **Love isn't enough**. Although we must love, love is not enough to survive: we must take action to show others we care—to *show* them we love. Yes: love is a verb.

3. **Happiness is not for sale**. We can't buy happiness, yet we search the aisles, shelves, and pages of eBay in search of something more—something to fill the void. The stuff won't make us happy, though—not in the long run, anyway. At best, material things will temporarily pacify us. At worst, it will ruin our lives, leaving us empty, depressed, and even more alone, alone among a sea of trinkets. The truth is we

are all going to die, and heaping our tombs with treasure will not save us from this fate.

4. **Success is perspectival**. I used to think I was successful because I had a six-figure job my friends and family could be proud of. I thought the house with too many bedrooms would make me look even more successful, as would the luxury car, the tailored suit, the expensive watch, the big screen TV, and all the trappings of the material world. I got it all, and I sure as hell didn't feel successful. Instead, I felt successfool.

5. **Make change a *must***. For the longest time, I knew I wanted to change: unhappy, unsatisfied, and unfulfilled, I knew I didn't have freedom. Not real freedom. The problem was I knew this *intellectually*, but not *emotionally*; I didn't have the feeling in my gut that things *must* change. I knew they *should* change, but the change wasn't a *must* for me, and thus it didn't happen. A decision is not a real decision until it is a *must*, until you feel it on your nerve-endings, until you are compelled to take action. Once your *shoulds* have turned into *musts*, then you are ready for change.

6. **The meaning of life**. Giving is living. The best way to live a worthwhile life is simple: continuously grow as an individual and contribute to other people in a meaningful way. Growth and contribution: that's the meaning of my life.

7. **Health is underestimated**. Our well-being is more important than most of us treat it: without health, nothing else matters.

8. **Sentimental items are less important**. My mother died

when I was 28. It was a difficult time in my life, but it helped me realize our memories aren't in our things: our memories are inside us.

9. **Your job is not your mission**. At least it wasn't for me, although I treated it like it was for the longest time. I worked so much that the rest of my life suffered. There's nothing wrong with hard work, as long as it doesn't get in the way of life's more important areas: health, relationships, passion.

10. **Finding your passion is important**. Passion is not preexisting, which means you can cultivate a passion as long as you find something that aligns with your principles and desires.

11. **Relationships matter**. Every relationship—friendship, romantic, or otherwise—is a series of gives and takes. Every relationship has an Us box. For the relationship to work, both people must contribute to—and get something from —that Us box. If you just give but don't get, you'll feel used, exploited, taken advantage of; if you only take but don't give, you're a parasite, a freeloader, a bottom-feeder.

12. **You don't need everyone to like you**. We all want to be loved—it's a mammalian instinct—but you can't value every relationship the same, and thus you can't expect everyone to love you the same. Life doesn't work that way. My friend Julien Smith articulates this sentiment very well in his popular essay "The Complete Guide to Not Giving a Fuck": "*When people don't like you, nothing actually happens. The world does not end. You don't feel them breathing down your neck. In fact, the more you ignore them and just go about your business, the better off you are.*"

13. **Status is a misnomer**. Similar to "success," our culture places an extraordinary emphasis on material wealth as a sign of true wealth, and yet I know too many people of supposed "status" who are miserable. They don't seem wealthy to me. One's true worth isn't determined by his or her net worth.

14. **Jealousy is a wasted emotion**. Competition breeds jealousy, although we often give it prettier labels like "competitive spirit" or "stick-to-itiveness" or "ambition." Jealousy is ugly, though: it is never a way to express we care—it's only a channel through which we broadcast our insecurities.

15. **Everybody worships something**. In his *This Is Water* commencement speech, my favorite fiction writer, David Foster Wallace, said it best: *"There is no such thing as not worshipping. Everybody worships. The only choice we get is what to worship."*

16. **I am not the center of the universe**. It's difficult to think about the world from a perspective other than our own. We are always worried about what's going on in our lives. What does my schedule look like today? What if I lose my job during the next round of layoffs? Why can't I stop smoking? Why am I overweight? Why am I not happy with my life? We are strongly aware of everything connected to our lives, but we are only one ingredient in a much larger recipe.

17. **Awareness is the most precious freedom**. Minimalism is a tool to rid ourselves of excess in favor of a deliberate life: it is a tool to take a seemingly intricate and convoluted world, cluttered with its endless embellishments, and make

it simpler, easier, realer. It is unimaginably hard to remain conscious, attentive, and aware. It is difficult not to fall back into a trance-like state, surrounded by the trappings and obstructions of the tiring world around us—but it is crucial to do so, for this is real freedom.

18. **Be on the mountain**. I use this term as a metaphor for living in the moment. When you climb to the peak, don't immediately plan your decent. Enjoy the view. *Be* on the mountain. Just *be*.

19. **We are scared for no reason**. Just ask yourself, "What am I afraid of?" We are often scared of things that don't have a real effect on our lives (or that we can't control, so we're worrying for no reason).

20. **Change is growth**. We all want a different outcome, and yet most of us don't want any change in our lives. Change equals uncertainty, and uncertainty equals discomfort, and discomfort isn't fun. But when we learn to enjoy the process of change—when we chose to look at uncertainty as *variety*—then we get to reap all the rewards of change. That is how we grow.

21. **Pretending to be perfect doesn't make us perfect**. I am not perfect, and I never will be. I make mistakes and bad decisions, and I fail at times. I stumble, I fall. I am human—a mixed bag, nuanced, the darkness and the light —as are you. And you are beautiful.

22. **The past does not equal the future**. My words are my words, and I can't take them back. You can't change the past, so it's important to focus on the present. If the past equaled the future, then your windshield would be of no

use to you: you would simply drive with your eyes glued to the rearview mirror. But driving this way—looking only behind you—is a surefire way to crash.

23. **Pain can be useful, but not suffering**. Pain lets us know something is wrong: it indicates we must change what we're doing. Suffering, though, is a choice, and we can choose to stop suffering, to learn a lesson from the pain and move on with our lives.

24. **Doubt kills**. The person who stops you from doing everything you want to do, who stops you from being completely free, who stops you from being healthy, happy, and passionate—is *you*.

25. **It's okay to wait**. Sometimes it's okay to wait a little longer for something. Why rush if you don't have to? Why not enjoy the journey?

26. **Honesty is important**. Honesty, at the most simple level, is telling the truth—not lying. It's supremely important to be honest, and it's hurtful when you're not, but:

27. **Openness is just as important as honesty**. Openness is more complicated than honesty: openness involves being honest while painting an accurate picture, shooting straight, not misleading other people, and being real. Openness is far more subjective, and you must be honest with yourself before you can be open with others. This doesn't mean you must put your entire life on display: some things are private, and that's okay, too.

28. **Getting people's buy-in**. Adding value to other people is the only way to get their buy-in. When I managed a large

team of people, I constantly asked them questions like, "How did you add value this week?" I also asked that question of myself, and I would share with my team how I added value that week. That's how I got their buy-in.

29. **Hype is cancerous**. So often we fall for the hype ("Buy More, Save More!" and "Three Day Sale!") and we are suckered into rash buying decisions because of scarcity and a false sense of urgency. We can train ourselves, though, to not only resist such hype, but to have a vitriolic reaction to the hype—to elicit a response so off-putting that we avoid anything that's hyped. When we're *aware* of the world around us, we can willfully develop a hype allergy.

30. **I'm still trying to figure it all out**. I don't intend to promulgate my views and opinions as some sort of maxims by which you should live your life. What works for me, might not work for you. Sometimes it doesn't even work for me.

For "30 More Life Lessons" by Ryan Nicodemus, visit TheMinimalists.com/30more.

I WILL ALWAYS BE OKAY

by Ryan Nicodemus

I will always be okay. *I will* always be successful. *I will* always be happy.

I will. Think about these two words for a moment. Life's revelations are found in the simplest of words: That's why most people will miss this. That's why some people who read this will brush it off as babble, as cliche, as a trite platitude.

If you can grasp these words and understand what I'm trying to convey, *you will* have the upper hand in life. And we all want control of our lives.

FIGHT CLUB'S TYLER DURDEN IS A MINIMALIST

Fight Club is not a film about fighting: it's a narrative about life, and getting rid of the corporate and cultural influences (or perhaps the confluence of the two) that control our lives. These are some of our favorite minimalist quotes from the film:

The things you own end up owning you.

It's only after we've lost everything that we're free to do anything.

You're not your job. You're not how much money you have in the bank. You're not the car you drive. You're not the contents of your wallet. You're not your fucking khakis. You're the all-singing, all-dancing crap of the world. [A note from Joshua: after re-reading this quote, I literally threw away every pair of khakis I owned. There was something about this quote, holistically, that had a real effect on my nerve endings.]

Reject the basic assumptions of civilization, especially the importance of material possessions.

Fuck off with your sofa units and strine green stripe

patterns, I say never be complete, I say stop being perfect, I say let … let's evolve, let the chips fall where they may.

The liberator who destroyed my property has realigned my perceptions.

Do you know what a duvet is? … It's a blanket. Just a blanket. Now why do guys like you and me know what a duvet is? Is this essential to our survival, in the hunter-gatherer sense of the word? No. What are we then? … We are consumers. We're the byproducts of a lifestyle obsession.

Murder, crime, poverty, these things don't concern me. What concerns me are celebrity magazines, television with 500 channels, some guy's name on my underwear. Rogaine, Viagra, Olestra … Fuck Martha Stewart. Martha's polishing the brass on the Titanic. It's all going down, man.

Man, I see in fight club the strongest and smartest men who've ever lived. I see all this potential, and I see squandering. God dammit, an entire generation pumping gas, waiting tables; slaves with white collars. Advertising has us chasing cars and clothes, working jobs we hate so we can buy shit we don't need. We're the middle children of history, man. No purpose or place. We have no Great War. No Great Depression. Our Great War's a spiritual war … our Great Depression is our lives. We've all been raised on television to believe that one day we'd all be millionaires, and movie gods, and rock stars. But we won't. And we're slowly learning that fact. And we're very, very pissed off.

What do you want? Wanna go back to the shit job, fucking condo world, watching sitcoms? Fuck you, I won't do it.

[Talking about consumerism] *We are all part of the same compost heap.*

How embarrassing … a house full of condiments and no food. [A metaphor for modern consumer driven life.]

[Narrator, while looking at a Calvin Klein-esque ad on the bus] *Is that what a real man is supposed to look like?*

Fuck what you know. You need to forget about what you know, that's your problem. Forget about what you think you know about life, about friendship, and especially about you and me.

Hitting bottom isn't a weekend retreat. It's not a goddamn seminar. Stop trying to control everything and just let go! LET GO!

Without pain, without sacrifice, we would have nothing.

Only after disaster can we be resurrected.

Guys, what would you wish you'd done before you died?

[After Raymond Hessel faces death but lives] *Tomorrow will be the most beautiful day of Raymond K. Hessel's life. His breakfast will taste better than any meal you and I have ever tasted.*

[Talking to himself about himself] *Hey, you created me … take some responsibility!*

[Talking about Fight Club] *And the eighth and final rule: if this is your first time at Fight Club, you have to fight.*

God Damn! We just had a near-life experience, fellas.
[Suggesting that most experiences are, by nature, dead.]

Sticking feathers up your butt does not make you a chicken.

Time to stand up for what you believe in.

If you are reading this then this warning is for you. Every word you read of this useless fine print is another second off your life. Don't you have other things to do? Is your life so empty that you honestly can't think of a better way to spend these moments? Or are you so impressed with authority that you give respect and credence to all that claim it? Do you read everything you're supposed to read? Do you think every thing you're supposed to think? Buy what you're told to want? Get out of your apartment. Meet a member of the opposite sex. Stop the excessive shopping and masturbation. Quit your job. Start a fight. Prove you're alive. If you don't claim your humanity you will become a statistic. You have been warned.

This is your life, and it's ending one minute at a time.

JEFFERSON'S 10 RULES FOR A GOOD LIFE

Was America's third president a minimalist? Probably not. We need only look at his 5,000-acre Monticello home, his cannonball-powered clocks, and his powdered wigs to assume simplicity was not on his mind. He did, however, have some compelling beliefs that align with our simple-living values. These are Thomas Jefferson's ten rules for a good life:

1. Never put off till tomorrow what you can do today.

2. Never trouble another for what you can do yourself.

3. Never spend your money before you have it.

4. Never buy what you do not want because it is cheap; it will never be dear to you.

5. Pride costs us more than hunger, thirst, and cold.

6. Never repent of having eaten too little.

7. Nothing is troublesome that we do willingly.

8. Don't let the evils that have never happened cost you pain.

9. Always take things by their smooth handle.

10. When angry, count to ten before you speak; if very angry, count to 100.

LIFE AFTER THE CRASH

by Ryan Nicodemus

You never know you're about to crash—until it's too late.

This winter, as I was driving the slushy interstate between Seattle and Missoula, a young man attempted to pass on my left. He suddenly lost control of his speeding vehicle. Terror set in. Everything transpired in slow motion. The air was Jell-O. Gravity was suspended. The man's car hydroplaned sideways into my lane.

Crash! My bumper collided with his passenger side. The high-speed impact forced us both toward the shoulder's steep decline.

"Everything's OK! Everything's OK! Everything's going to be OK!" I attempted to convince my girlfriend, Mariah, wide-eyed in the passenger seat. We slid off the road. Inertia forced both vehicles forward. Our car began to roll.

Everything was fine just a few seconds before. After spending a few days skiing in Canada, Mariah and I were driving back to Montana—smiling, laughing, singing off-key renditions of 80s songs. A breath later everything changed. Our car flipped and tumbled toward the ravine.

Thankfully, other than a few bruises and sore muscles, we were fine. Most important—we're alive. Had we not been wearing our safety belts, though, you'd be reading our obituaries.

My life didn't flash before my eyes during this near-death experience, but I did have a revelation as everything collided and careened in slow motion—a revelation I didn't expect: *If I die today, I've lived an outstanding life. I've done nearly everything I set out to do with my time here on earth.*

I couldn't have said this two years ago. Now I can, which means the rest of my post-crash life is bonus time—and the key is to determine how to best spend those years.

Any of us could die today. Right now. So everything after this moment is a gift. How can we best spend our bonus time, then? Shopping? Browsing Facebook? Working hard for a paycheck to buy stuff that won't make us happy?

Or maybe by living more deliberately, focused on the people around us? Maybe by creating more and consuming less?

The good news is these bonus hours are *ours*: we get to decide.

LIVE LIKE STAN

by Joshua Fields Millburn

The traffic light above our car is a blur of red. Tears burn my eyes. Ryan is in the passenger seat. He, too, is teary-eyed. It's the eve of our big, 100-city book tour. The Florida sun has already set behind the Tampa Bay. Nightfall is upon us. By the time the traffic light changes, it's a mess of wet green, a shapeless emerald cloud spilling into the nighttime ether.

I received the call a minute earlier: a week after Ryan avoided his own death, one of my closest friends, Stanley Dukes, is dead.

This isn't going to be easy to write. Overwhelmed with unanswerable questions, I feel a canyon of sorrow. I can't see past the tears. He was only 36, so I'm compelled to pen a thousand cliches:

Life is too short.
Every day is a gift.
You never know when you're going to go, so live your life to the fullest.

While all these truisms are apt, the truth is Stan lived more in his three and half decades than most people could in 100 years. Stanley Dukes was a Mozart of positive living, and so his attenuated life was not in vain. This doesn't erase the pain, but it makes it easier to handle.

We met in the corporate world a decade ago. At first, when I was a regional manager, Stan worked for me as a store manager, but he was so talented—he added so much value to so many lives—that I often felt I worked for him. Though he managed dozens of employees, his genius was most pronounced in his ability to inspire people who weren't self-motivated, which, if you know anything about leading people, is like convincing water to be less wet. Somehow he did it, though, always carrying with him a smile and his "PMA" (Positive Mental Attitude). As a result, he was one of the most successful managers in the company.

We became close friends. We shared similar values and beliefs, as well as tastes in literature, movies, and music: I traded him my overwrought short stories for his hilarious pseudonymous erotic fiction, we exchanged lines from *Glengarry Glen Ross* characters, and we both shared a healthy obsession for John Mayer's music. We became so close he is the first person to make an appearance in our memoir, *Everything That Remains*, where he pops his huge, lovable head into the very first page:

Our identities are shaped by the costumes we wear. I am seated in a cramped conference room, surrounded by ghosts in shirtsleeves and pleated trousers. There are 35, maybe 40, people here. Middle managers, the lot of us. Mostly Caucasian, mostly male, all oozing apathy. The group's median complexion is that of an agoraphobe. A Microsoft Excel spreadsheet is projected onto an oversized canvas pulled from the ceiling at the front of the room. The canvas is flimsy and cracked and is a shade of off-white that suggests it's a relic from a time when employees were allowed to smoke indoors. The rest of the room is aggressively white: the walls are white, the ceiling is white, the people are white, as if all cut from the same materials. Well, everyone except Stan, seated at the back of the room. Cincinnati's population is forty-five percent black, but Stan is part of our company's single-digit percentage. His comments, rarely solicited by executives, are oft-dismissed with a nod and a pained smile. Although he's the size of an NFL linebacker, Stan is a paragon of kindness. But that doesn't stop me from secretly hoping that one day he'll get fed up with the patronizing grins and make it his duty to reformat one of the bosses' fish-eyed faces.

Stan never would've touched a hair on any of their balding heads—he was above that. He was above all the petty bullshit we get caught up in every day. He was above living life based on other people's standards: his standards were too high for that. He had character.

Stan contributed beyond himself. Each year at Christmastime, he dressed up as "Stanta" and handed out gifts to our employees. He spent many off hours donating his time to soup kitchens and Habitat for Humanity. In his last year he founded a mentorship conference for young men ages thirteen to eighteen.

Stan cared. When I decided to leave the corporate world, he didn't flinch—he was the first to join me. We walked away together, guided by solidarity and a kinship that's impossible to manufacture. Before I moved to Montana, we met for coffee weekly. Our visits yielded heartfelt advice on women and life, as well as arguments over which album was John Mayer's best (*Heavier Things* or *Battle Studies*?). Everything about Stan reflected a profound Truth. Even his simple tweets were steeped in profundity:

> *A man can't walk out of his own story.*
> *Secure your own mask before assisting others.*
> *There's a bright spot in every shadow.*
> *The bitter allows me to appreciate the sweet.*
> *Don't drown in conformity.*
> *Only your actions prove your worth: they tell people who you are.*

Countless essays in this book were inspired by my conversations with Stan. Our final conversation was mimetic of his life: it was short, but meaningful. Three days before Thanksgiving I sent him a message: "I don't have to wait till Thursday to be thankful for you. I'm grateful you're in my life." To which he succinctly replied: "Thanks. Know I feel the same."

Stan *lived* until he died. Truly lived. Every day. Not like most of us who walk through life like it's some kind of dress rehearsal, worrying about bullshit that just doesn't matter. No—Stan was so alive, one of the only people I know who didn't take this life for granted.

If there's a lesson to be learned here, it's that, like Stan, we're all going to die—but few of us will be courageous enough to live as he did: honest, well-rounded, passionate, positive, and constantly improving. Above all, Stan Dukes was good people, a man I aspire to *live* like.

That green blur overhead is my signal to step on the gas, to wipe the tears, to move forward. Perhaps you'll do likewise. I know Stan would.

ABOUT THE MINIMALISTS

JOSHUA FIELDS MILLBURN & RYAN NICODEMUS are bestselling authors and international speakers who write and speak about living a meaningful life with less stuff. Their books include *Essential: Essays by The Minimalists*, *Minimalism: Live a Meaningful Life*, *As a Decade Fades: A Novel*, and *Everything That Remains: A Memoir*. They have been featured in the *New York Times*, *Wall Street Journal*, *USA Today*, *Forbes*, *Boston Globe*, *San Francisco Chronicle*, *Chicago Tribune*, *Seattle Times*, *Toronto Star*, *Globe & Mail*, *Vancouver Sun*, *Village Voice*, *LA Weekly*, and many other outlets. Visit the authors online at TheMinimalists.com.